MINDFULNESS
IN EIGHT WEEKS

This book is a real joy ... Michael has laid it out clearly, succinctly and approachably. It's a wonderful mix of clear, practical guidance and sound scientific evidence. Read this book, follow and practise the guidance, and enjoy the fruits!

Rebecca Crane, Director, Centre for
Mindfulness Research and Practice, Bangor University

Before I met Michael I thought I knew all there was to know about my thoughts. I was wrong.
  Eight weeks on I knew a feeling of space and calm. The internal chatter of my mind was there but not so demanding or noisy. Instead, I was just enjoying a new sense of seeing the world as it is rather than as the setting for my own thoughts.

David Sillito, Media and Arts Correspondent, BBC

This book provides a highly accessible way for people to learn mindfulness, experience its potential to relieve suffering, and cultivate joy, compassion and wisdom.

Willem Kuyken, Professor of Clinical Psychology, Exeter University

Mindfulness in Eight Weeks is a clear, practical and wise companion as you embark on the journey of transformation outlined in the book's programme. With its balance of scientific knowledge, detailed meditation instructions and tips on how to bring mindfulness into daily life, it is indeed a trustworthy and accessible manual as, step by step, you change your mind and change your life.

Vidyamala Burch, Author and co-founder of Breathworks CIC

As we campaign in Parliament and in government to raise awareness of the benefits of mindfulness training more generally, I hope this new book will open many more eyes to the great benefits that are so readily available with mindfulness practice.

Chris Ruane MP

THE REVOLUTIONARY EIGHT-WEEK PLAN
TO CLEAR YOUR MIND AND CALM YOUR LIFE

MINDFULNESS
IN EIGHT WEEKS

MICHAEL CHASKALSON

HARPER
thorsons

HarperThorsons
An imprint of HarperCollins*Publishers*
1 London Bridge Street, London SE1 9GF

www.harpercollins.co.uk

First published by HarperThorsons 2014

13

A catalogue record of this book is
available from the British Library

PB ISBN 978-0-00-759143-5
EB ISBN 978-0-00-759144-2

Printed and bound in Great Britain by
CPI Group (UK) Ltd, Croydon CR0 4YY

CONTENTS

INTRODUCTION

MINDFULNESS IS EVERYWHERE

When I first started practising mindfulness in the UK back in the 1970s, very few people outside of Asia had heard of it. Now it's everywhere. *TIME Magazine* devoted a recent cover to it, US congressmen and British Members of Parliament are vocal about its benefits, public courses abound, there are widely respected programmes available for schoolchildren and young adults, the US Marines are building it into their training, top corporations offer training in it to their employees, scientists study its effects (there are around 40 peer-reviewed scientific papers on the theme published every month) and NICE, the UK's National Institute for Health and Clinical Excellence that advises the UK National Health Service on appropriate treatments, recommends an eight-week mindfulness course as a front-line intervention for certain conditions.

Almost every week another mainstream publication, a magazine or newspaper, carries an article that speaks of the popularity of mindfulness and its apparent benefits, and there seems to be an unending stream of books about it.

SO WHY ANOTHER BOOK?

Because it's one thing just to read about mindfulness and quite another thing to practise it. The aim of this book is to support you in its actual practice. You can use the book as a do-it-yourself manual for learning mindfulness in a structured way or you can use it to supplement the teaching on a teacher-led eight-week mindfulness programme. You can also use it simply to find out more about the approach and to try some of the ideas and practices for yourself.

The book is built around an eight-week mindfulness course that is a combination of the two most popular and widely researched mindfulness approaches – Mindfulness-Based Stress Reduction (MBSR) and Mindfulness-Based Cognitive Therapy (MBCT). However you use this book, you will get the most from it by actually trying out some of the mindfulness practices taught here over a period of time.

My intention is for this book to be practical and – as much as possible in this medium – experiential. Although I will refer from time to time to the considerable scientific research into the effects of mindfulness training and I will be discussing some of the theory that underlies the approach, all of that is intended to support and illuminate the actual *practice* of mindfulness. The true meaning of mindfulness emerges ultimately from its practice and that is something you have to do for yourself. In the end, it is only by practising some of the methods of mindfulness that you can discover their real significance and begin to share in the very considerable benefits that they offer. Those benefits *are* really considerable – so many and various – and are accessible to people in a wide variety of contexts.

I teach mindfulness in many different settings these days. My associates and I run public self-enrolment eight-week mindfulness courses in London and elsewhere. We also bring programmes like the one outlined here to people in organisations – banks, Internet companies, media organisations, financial and professional services companies, the UK's National Health Service and so on. I work with large groups or one-to-one with senior staff. I've taught people working at senior board level in large global organisations and I've worked in a space littered with potting compost teaching a course to the staff who run a plant nursery alongside clients who have learning difficulties. Sometimes we teach the full eight-week programme, sometimes we deliver a shorter introduction. We teach Mindfulness for Leaders courses and we teach mindfulness for general staff. But, however or wherever we teach, the basic premise of the work remains the same: when you're more skilled at working with your mind and mental states things go better for you and for those around you.

After training in mindfulness myself for around 40 years now, and teaching others for much of that time, I feel I can say this unequivocally – mindfulness works.

HOW TO USE THIS BOOK

The heart of this book is an eight-week mindfulness training course, and that is reflected in its structure. Each chapter comprises instructions for a particular set of practices that you can engage in that week. The practices are cumulative and follow one another in a particular order – building from week to week.

The core course material is laid out in one consistent style. All the other material – apart from the home practice – can be thought of as somewhat optional reading. These breakout boxes are marked with different icons:

The icon 🧭 tells you that a box contains instruction and guidance that are necessary for the course.

The icon 💡 shows that the box contains ideas that I'll be referring to as the course unfolds.

The icon 🏠 shows that the box contains a description of the set home practice for this week.

The icon *i* lets you know that the box marked by it

contains useful information that is not absolutely necessary for you to know as you follow the course. Read it if you're interested, or skip it if you'd rather.

The icon (📖) tells you that the box contains a poem or a story that further illustrates some of the points being made in that chapter.

I have also provided downloadable audio materials to support each week's mindfulness practice. These can be found at www.mbsr.co.uk/mp31.php. There are two streams of daily practice that you can follow. The first stream follows the home-practice pathway of 'classic' MBSR and MBCT in suggesting that you do at least 40 minutes of home practice each day. Most of the research findings showing significant changes as a result of engaging in MBSR or MBCT have been based on a daily practice programme similar to this.

If you're using this book as part of a teacher-led group-based eight-week course, do follow Stream 1 home practice unless your instructor suggests otherwise.

Having said all that, I'm aware that undertaking 40 minutes a day of home practice, especially without the support of a group, can be a real challenge. For that reason I've devised a second stream of practice. Stream 2 home practice takes no more than 20 minutes each day and may be useful for those who are using the book alone to guide their mindfulness training and who don't have regular access to a teacher-led group.

The daily practice programme for each week of the course is laid out at the end of the chapter for each week, and Stream 1 and Stream 2 home-practice guidance is clearly delineated.

Finally, if you're using the book as part of a teacher-led course, you'll get the most from that course if, once you've read this introductory chapter, you leave any further reading until *after* you have participated in that week's class with the teacher. Try to avoid reading ahead – it can undermine the effects of the work you'll be doing on the course itself.

HOME PRACTICE IS ESSENTIAL

As you'll see from the outcomes described in the book, with regular daily mindfulness practice real changes are possible. What is on offer here is a significant increase in your level of well-being and personal effectiveness. I'm personally committed to teaching mindfulness and I'm inspired to do that because I see real changes taking place from week to week in the people I work with. It's not always a smooth journey. There are ups and downs and we tell people on our public courses that engaging in the stress-reduction courses we offer can sometimes be stressful. After all, for many people these days finding 10 minutes a day to fit in the practices really isn't easy. But practice is what this is all about and, if you commit to your stream of practice and do it with whatever regularity you can muster, real change can follow.

And here's the really wonderful thing: as you set out on your journey into mindfulness you don't have to try to change yourself. In fact, striving after results can inhibit the process. All you have to do is engage in the practices – again and again and again – and change will begin to emerge. Over time, some people find that, once they have begun to experience for themselves the attitude of kindly self-acceptance that lies at the heart of this programme, they want to engage in further processes of development which build on that foundation. In the 'Further Resources' section (see page 247) I discuss a few of the many options that may be available, but for now the main thing is simply to engage in the practices described for each week. As best you can, put aside any idea of getting them right or doing them perfectly. That striving attitude is perfectly normal, it's part of our being human, but in this context it just gets in the way.

Don't strive to get the practices right. Just do them.

And here's another great thing. On this course you're completely liberated from any obligation to enjoy the practices. Sometimes you may enjoy them, sometimes you may not. That's not the point. You don't need to enjoy them to get the benefit – but you do have to do them.

WHAT EXACTLY DO WE MEAN BY MINDFULNESS?

Mindfulness is not the same thing as meditation. Meditation, especially 'mindfulness meditation', is a method of practice whose outcome is intended to be greater mindfulness.

Mindfulness is the quality of awareness that comes from paying attention to yourself, others and the world around you in a certain way. Jon Kabat-Zinn (of whom more later) speaks of it as the awareness that arises from paying attention on purpose, in the present moment and non-judgementally.

Let's look at that in more detail.

Mindfulness Involves Paying Attention on Purpose

The act of choosing to pay attention is rarer than you might at first think. Even as you're reading these words, how attentive are you? For most of us, the act of reading is fairly automatic. An impulse moves us to pick up a book, we open it, begin to read . . . and all the while our attention flits.

This is neither right nor wrong – it's just how we are, and even as you have read just these few pages so far, part of your mind will quite naturally have wandered off many times to engage with other things that call on your attention. Maybe part of your mind spent some time turning over a problem at work or at home. Maybe you thought for a bit about some of the tasks on your to-do list right now. Or perhaps something you read sparked a memory and an image from the past came vividly to mind. Maybe you began to think about your next meal and you ran through a quick inventory of one of your kitchen cupboards.

As I said, none of this is right or wrong. It's just how our minds work. And when we're mindful we bring a much clearer intentionality and awareness to the process of paying attention. When we're mindful, we choose – to some extent at least – where our attention goes. We pay attention *on purpose*.

Mindfulness Involves Paying Attention in the Present Moment

Our attention wanders and much of the time it wanders off into the past or into the future. Sometimes there are elements of anxiety or regret involved in this. We may look to the future with a kind of anxious anticipation for what is to come, maintaining an uneasy alertness by constantly scanning the future for the challenges it may bring: encounters with other people we must prepare for, tasks we need to tick off our list – stuff coming our way. Or we may find ourselves constantly reviewing the past, especially the things we regret. There might even be some unconscious sense that by doing so we'll be better prepared for the future.

Perhaps there are evolutionary processes at work here. Maybe we've survived as a species and become the planet's top predators in part because we're good at doing these things. But there is a price for this and that price may be the whole of our lives. If your attention is always in the future or always in the past, right now you're simply not here. Right now, you're not fully alive.

When you're mindful, your attention stays in the present moment. Right here, right now.

Mindfulness Is Non-Judgemental

This doesn't mean that we don't make judgements when we're mindful, or that we stop discerning what is appropriate at any time from what is inappropriate. That would be simple foolishness. But think of what we mean when we speak of someone being 'judgemental'. A thesaurus gives these synonyms: critical, hypercritical, condemnatory, negative, disapproving, disparaging, pejorative. Quite a list.

The non-judgemental attitude of mindfulness, on the other hand, is neither condemnatory nor prejudicial. There are two dimensions to this.

Firstly, there is what we might think of as a *wisdom* dimension. This involves letting what *is* the case *be* the case.

Much of the time we may feel, instinctively almost, unwilling or unable to do this. We can put huge amounts of mental and emotional energy into refusing to allow things to simply be as they are. 'They shouldn't be like that!' 'It shouldn't be like this!' 'I ought to be somehow different . . .' But things really only ever are as they actually are. However right, however wrong, however just or unjust, desirable or undesirable – they are as they are. And it's only ever when we can allow this to be fact – that things are as they are – that choice can begin to open up for us. When we let what *is* the case *be* the case, whatever it is, then we can begin to choose how to respond to it. What shall we do about what's showed up right now? What would be the most appropriate next step for us and for the situation as a whole?

When we can't let what *is* the case *be* the case, then we're stuck. We're already rooted in a defensive posture of denial and we've closed down the possibilities for a more creative engagement with the situation. The *wisdom* element in the non-judgemental attitude of mindfulness opens up the possibility for a more wholehearted creative response to the situations we find ourselves in. It allows for more creative choices.

Then, there is a *compassion* dimension to the non-judgemental attitude of mindfulness. Here, to some extent at least, we still our inner critical voice.

For much of the time, many of us find that we run a kind of inner critical commentary on our experience. Sometimes that commentary can be directed at ourselves — 'I'm not good enough.' 'I don't measure up.'

How many of us actually think we're thin enough, good-looking enough, smart enough, fit enough, strong enough, witty enough, rich enough, clever enough, fast enough . . . anything enough?

Sometimes we turn that inner critical commentary on others — on their appearance, their intelligence, their emotional appropriateness and so on. Sometimes we run critical commentaries on our immediate environment — somehow or other, in one way or another, things just aren't right. Nothing is quite as it should be. Nothing, ourselves included, is quite enough.

The compassion element in the non-judgemental attitude of mindfulness allows us to rest simply with things as they are — at least to some extent. We allow ourselves to be ourselves, we allow others to be who they are, and we rest a little bit more at ease with life as it actually is — with a bit more kindly acceptance towards ourselves, others and the world around us.

The quality of acceptance that emerges from mindfulness training isn't simple passivity, however. It's not that we passively allow the world to roll over us, or that we stop making ethical judgements. Far from it. Mindfulness training might even enable you to be more appropriately assertive. It might sharpen your capacity for drawing ethical distinctions. But all of this can be done with wisdom and with kindness.

With mindfulness training you begin to develop a greater

capacity to allow what is the case to be the case and to respond skilfully and appropriately with a warm open-heartedness.

BOX 1: A SMALL DIGRESSION INTO HISTORY

This book is based on a completely secular approach to mindfulness training. It is for people of any religion or none. For 2,500 years, however, the ideas and practices at the core of the approach were found almost exclusively in Buddhist monasteries in Asia. So far as we're aware, the Buddha was the first person in history to use the idea of mindfulness as we use it in contemporary mindfulness approaches. He taught a number of mindfulness practices and other methods for developing and sustaining mindfulness and he spoke at length of the immense benefits that are on offer from engaging in those practices. That approach and a body of teachings and practices that came from it lived on in a wide variety of Buddhist monastic contexts in Asia but, for 2,500 years, people outside of Asia knew almost nothing about it.

Towards the end of the nineteenth century that began to change as European explorers, scholars and colonial administrators began to discover and translate into their own contexts some of what was going on in Asian monasteries. At first, only a tiny handful of these took up the practices for themselves, and the penetration of mindfulness approaches into European and North American culture was slow and gradual. But it built steadily and received a boost in the 1950s with the emergence of the Beats – poets and writers like Allen Ginsberg, Jack Kerouac and Gary Snyder, who began to publicly advocate the practice. It received more of a boost in the 1960s and 1970s with the psychedelic movement, when people like myself – hippies and wannabe hippies – began to get involved. But mindfulness practices were still largely to be found only in Buddhist contexts.

Towards the end of the 1970s, however, a very significant shift took place. Much of this comes down to Jon Kabat-Zinn. Jon had trained as a molecular biologist and was working as such at a hospital near Boston – the University of Massachusetts (UMass) Medical Center. In his student days he had come upon Buddhism and had established a regular daily meditation practice. Apart from his work at the hospital, he also taught yoga. He engaged with his scientific work, but two other questions kept bothering him. One question he expressed as 'What shall I do with my life? What kind of work do I love so much I would pay to do it?' The other was more to do with the patients who came to the hospital.

He saw that people came to the hospital because, in one way or another, they were suffering. But how many of them, he wondered, left the hospital with that suffering resolved? In discussion with physicians at the hospital he came to the conclusion that it was maybe something like 20 per cent of patients. What, he wondered, was the system offering to the other 80 per cent?

While on a silent meditation retreat in 1979 these two streams of questioning resolved themselves in a 'vision' lasting maybe 10 seconds, which Jon describes as an instantaneous seeing of vivid, almost inevitable connections and their implications.

He recognised in that moment that the way he was working on that retreat on his own mind and mental states might have enormous benefits for the people who came to the hospital with their suffering. He saw that it might be possible to share the essence of the meditation and yoga teachings that he had been practising for the past 13 years with those who might never come to a Buddhist centre, and who would never be able to discover that essence through the words and forms that were used in such places. He resolved to try to make the practices and the language used to describe them so commonsensical that anyone might benefit from them.

Jon persuaded the hospital authorities to let him and his colleagues have some space in the basement, and there they developed what soon came to be known as the eight-week Mindfulness-Based Stress Reduction (MBSR) programme. He and his colleagues worked to develop a contemporary vocabulary that spoke to the heart of the matter without reference to the cultural aspects of the traditions out of which those practices emerged.

Jon had trained as a scientist and knew the value of research, so he and his colleagues researched the patient outcomes of their programme and, bit by bit, what is now a very considerable body of research evidence into the efficacy of the training began to emerge. At the time of writing there are many thousands of peer-reviewed scientific papers investigating the effects of mindfulness training. If you're interested in these, you'll find an extensive database of them at www.mindfulexperience.org.

It soon became clear that MBSR training enabled people to deal much better with chronic pain. They also became more adept at managing the various stressors that accompanied whatever issues had brought them to the hospital. The research indicates that the programme is successful at helping people deal with difficulty and, at the time of writing, more than 20,000 people have completed the eight-week course at UMass itself. More than 740 academic medical centres, hospitals, clinics and freestanding programmes offer MBSR to the public around the world, and interest in mindfulness training has continued to build as it has become increasingly apparent that it is not only stress and chronic pain that are positively affected when you learn to work with your attention in a different way.

Biological changes started to show up in the research as well. One early instance of this was the finding that, among patients who came to the hospital for treatment for psoriasis, the symptoms of those who engaged in the MBSR course alongside that treatment cleared up around 50 per cent faster than the symptoms of patients who didn't. What this seemed to show was that what people were doing with their minds, the work they were doing with their attention, was actually changing their bodies.

The understanding of the way in which mindfulness training affects us biologically received a further boost when neuroscientists began to investigate its effects.

Part of this story goes back to 1992, when a small group of neuroscientists led by Professor Richard Davidson and helped by Alan Wallace, a Western Buddhist scholar, travelled to Dharamsala in the foothills of the Indian Himalayas on a kind of neuroscience expedition. They took with them an array of what was then cutting-edge scientific equipment: laptop computers, electroencephalographs, battery packs and a generator. They wanted to meet some of the Tibetan Buddhist hermit-meditators who lived in the hills above the town and they hoped to recruit from among them a cohort of expert meditators – people who had put in tens of thousands of hours of meditation practice. The neuroscientists wanted to study the pattern of their brain activity. They were particularly interested in the habits of thinking and feeling they exhibited when not meditating. If these demonstrated that the subjects had unusual habitual traits, these might reflect enduring functional changes that had occurred in their brains as a result of their mental training.

This first foray simply failed. To begin with, the yogis were unimpressed by what seemed to them to be the scientists' uninformed and naïve perspectives on meditation. 'We seemed like primitive Neanderthals to them,' explained Alan Wallace, who helped to facilitate the encounters.

In the end the scientists got no usable data from that trip. But they'd made a start and, with the Dalai Lama's help, in 2001 a number of maroon-robed Tibetan Buddhist monks began to make their way to Davidson's Laboratory for Affective Neuroscience in Madison, Wisconsin, to meditate with EEG caps stuck on their already shaven heads. These were 'Olympic-level athletes' of meditation, with many years of intensive practice behind them. The results were astounding. The expert meditators exhibited patterns of brain activity never before measured by science. We'll look in more detail at some of these findings in Week Three. They're particularly interesting because from them scientists were encouraged to investigate what changes might show up in people who had no previous meditation experience and who took up an eight-week mindfulness training course. Here, they found (and research continues to find) highly significant changes in the patterns of brain activation – and even changes in the brain's physical structure – that follow from just eight weeks of mindfulness training.

BOX 2: MINDFULNESS-BASED COGNITIVE THERAPY

A significant event in the development of secular mindfulness training came about in 1992 when three distinguished cognitive psychologists – Zindel Segal, Mark Williams and John Teasdale – were asked by the director of a clinical psychology research network to develop a group-based therapy for the treatment of relapsing depression.

Significant depression is a highly disabling condition. Besides emotional pain and anguish, people who are depressed also experience levels of functional impairment comparable to those found in major medical illnesses – including cancer and coronary heart disease – and a World Health Organization projection suggests that of all diseases depression will impose the second-largest burden of ill health worldwide by the year 2020.

Roughly one in 10 of us in Europe and North America will experience serious depression at some point in our lives. In some parts of the population that is more like one in four. What is more, when people have had three or more serious episodes of depression there is something like a 67 per cent chance that their depression will relapse.

Back in 1992, the two treatments that seemed to be most effective in treating people with relapsing depression were one-to-one cognitive behaviour therapy (CBT) or maintenance doses of antidepressants. Both of these are relatively expensive. Not everyone is comfortable taking the drugs and they can have unwanted side effects. And not everyone can have one-to-one CBT – there is a limit to the availability of trained therapists. Coming up with an economically viable and effective group-based intervention therefore seemed urgent.

To understand the approach Segal, Williams and Teasdale took, and why they took it, it will be helpful to consider a scenario they outline in the first of their books – *Mindfulness-Based Cognitive Therapy for Depression*.

Mary has just come from work. She's tired and she looks forward to spending her evening relaxing in front of the television. However, there's a message on her answerphone. Her partner is going to be late getting back from work. She gets angry and feels disappointed and upset. Then she starts to recall other occasions that month when the same thing happened. She begins to imagine that her partner may be being unfaithful to her. She pushes that thought to one side but it comes back with even greater force when she imagines that she has heard some laughter in the background of his voicemail. Nausea comes up – and it doesn't end there. Her mind rapidly starts to conjure up images of an unwanted future – solicitors, divorce courts, having to buy another home, living in poverty. She feels herself getting more and more upset as her anger begins to turn into depression. Her mind throws up images from the past when she was rejected and lonely. She 'knows' that all their mutual friends would abandon her for him. Tears flow as she is left wondering what to do. Sitting in her kitchen she asks herself 'Why does this always happen to me?' and she tries to work out why she always reacts this way.

Mary experiences a whole avalanche of thoughts, feelings and sensations. It is not just the negative matter that caused her to be upset, however, nor is it just the way she found herself trying to deal with it. Instead, it's as if a whole *mode of mind* – a complex configuration of moods, thoughts, images, impulses and body sensations – was very quickly wheeled into place in response to the situation. This mode of mind includes both the negative material *and* Mary's tendency to deal with it by ruminating.

Like Mary, people who are vulnerable to depression can put much of their time and energy into ruminating about their experience – 'Why do I feel the way I do?' Thinking about their problems, their sense of personal inadequacy, they turn things over and over in their minds trying to think their way to solutions and to ways of reducing their distress. But, as Segal, Williams and Teasdale point out, the methods they use to achieve that aim are tragically counterproductive. In fact, when you're low, repeatedly ruminating – thinking about apparently negative aspects of yourself or of problematic situations – actively perpetuates rather than resolves depression.

What seems to happen is that, at times of low mood, old habits of thinking switch in relatively automatically. That has two consequences: firstly, thinking now runs in well-worn grooves that don't lead to a way out of depression; secondly, this way of thinking itself intensifies the depressed mood – and that leads to further rumination. In this way a series of self-perpetuating vicious cycles can cause mild and transient low mood to very quickly degenerate into severe, disabling depression.

As Segal, Williams and Teasdale saw it, the task of relapse prevention was therefore to find a way to help patients disengage from negative and self-perpetuating rumination when they felt sad or at other times of potential relapse.

While they were pursuing these questions, John Teasdale, who had long had a personal interest in meditation, was reminded of a Buddhist talk he had attended several years before where the speaker stressed that it is not your experience itself that makes you unhappy – it is your *relationship* to that experience. This is a central aspect of mindfulness meditation, in which you learn – among other things – to relate to your thoughts just as thoughts. In other words, you learn to see them just as mental events, rather than as 'the truth' or 'me'.

John recognised that this way of 'decentring' from negative thoughts, of standing ever so slightly apart from them and witnessing them as an *aspect* of experience rather being completely immersed in them as the whole of experience, might be a key.

But how could you teach people to do that?

An American colleague, Marsha Linehan, who was visiting John Teasdale and Mark Williams at the Medical Research Council's Applied Psychology Unit in Cambridge, provided a vital clue. Besides telling them of her own work in helping patients to decentre, she pointed them towards the work being undertaken at UMass by Jon Kabat-Zinn. Looking into his work, they came upon this piece from one of Jon's books:

> It is remarkable how liberating it feels to be able to see that your thoughts are just thoughts and that they are not 'you' or 'reality' . . . The simple act of recognising your thoughts as *thoughts* can free you from the distorted reality they often create and allow for more clear-sightedness and a greater sense of manageability in your life.

Segal, Williams and Teasdale made contact with Kabat-Zinn and his Stress Reduction Clinic at the UMass Medical Center, began to engage in various ways with his programme and, based largely upon it, formulated their own eight-week Mindfulness-Based Cognitive Therapy (MBCT) programme. Although similar to Kabat-Zinn's Mindfulness-Based Stress Reduction (MBSR) in many ways, MBCT contains elements of cognitive therapy and theory that address the specific vulnerabilities and exacerbating factors that make depression recurrent.

MBCT itself was originally specifically designed for those vulnerable to depression. Subsequently, variants of it have been developed to help with a wide range of issues: obsessive-compulsive disorder, disordered eating, addiction, traumatic brain injury, obesity and bipolar disorder among others.

When it comes to depression, the results of several large-scale randomised control trials suggest that, for people vulnerable to relapsing depression, a course of MBCT might more or less halve the rate of relapse and, if relapse does occur, those who have trained in MBCT appear to experience it less severely.

BOX 3: HOW DID THE COURSE AT THE HEART OF THIS BOOK COME TO BE FORMULATED?

My Own History with Mindfulness
I come to this work from a Buddhist background. Born in South Africa and unable to reconcile myself to the apartheid regime, I left there at eighteen and settled in England. Driven to find a framework of values I could depend on and an understanding of how the world worked, I took up a degree in philosophy at the University of East Anglia in Norwich. But that didn't really fulfil my

need. In my final year, though, I had the good fortune to meet a committed practising Buddhist who had come to town to establish a Buddhist centre. He taught me to meditate and that changed everything. I committed to spending the rest of my life devoted to meditation, study, retreat and eventually to teaching others.

I lived sometimes in retreat centres, sometimes in city-based residential Buddhist communities, and gradually came to teach and to publish books on Buddhism (using my Buddhist name – Kulananda), and I thought that was how my life was going to go. For several years I took a kind of digression into the world of business. With a number of Buddhist friends I came to establish a 'right livelihood' fair-trade company that dealt in handicrafts from developing countries. The company came to be quite successful in time. At the peak of its success it employed around 200 people, had sales of around £10 million a year and gave its profits – often substantial sums – to various Buddhist charities each year. But running a business turned out not to be what I really wanted to do with myself and in 1988 I returned to a life based more in teaching, studying and meditating.

By 2002, however, more than 25 years after my first introduction to meditation, I began to feel the need to make another change and I looked about for a form of training that would build on my existing skills but which would allow me to earn a living in the world. I thought about training in psychotherapy. After all, I'd had many years doing informal pastoral counselling. Searching one day on the Internet, I came upon a master's degree programme that was being run at Bangor University in Wales. The programme had originally been founded by Professor Mark Williams, one of the founders of MBCT, with the intention of training up a number of people who could begin to bring mindfulness into various clinical settings. That seemed like a marriage made in heaven to me. I joined the programme and graduated from it in 2006.

Reading *Mindfulness-Based Cognitive Therapy for Depression* – one of the set texts at Bangor – was a profound revelation for me. Here, for the first time, I saw the coming together of two great streams of tradition: Buddhist psychology, which implicitly informs much of what is found in that book, and Western psychology, founded in the tradition of scientific method, which explicitly informs it. Traditional Buddhist psychology, at its best, is founded on a detailed and scholarly investigation of the elements of experience revealed by a collective endeavour of deep introspection over more than 1,000 years. Plunging in meditation into the depths of their own minds, the founding scholars of Buddhist psychology provide us with profoundly valuable insights into the mechanisms of consciousness and the functioning of perception and experience. Western psychology at its best, on the other hand, brings a highly sophisticated scientific method and a well-developed scientific community to its investigations.

In *Mindfulness-Based Cognitive Therapy for Depression* I saw the first beginnings of what might be achieved as these two streams began to inform one another. I was deeply inspired by the way the authors illuminated some of the inner psychological processes at work in the client group they were concerned with. When we understand the processes that drive us and that make up our experience, we have a much greater chance of freeing ourselves from their unconscious grip. The intersection of mindfulness and Western science, I saw, opened up huge possibilities for human development and human freedom.

Besides relishing the psychological acuity I was discovering, I was also deeply inspired by the explicitly secular nature of the trainings offered by MBSR and MBCT. Ever since discovering mindfulness and related practices for myself I have held a passionate conviction that they offer something deeply lacking in contemporary society. Here, at last, was a vehicle for getting some of these practices and their benefits out into the wider world without any strings attached. I love the freedom and openness of that offering. You don't need to be a Buddhist or subscribe to any religious framework to get these benefits now. What previously had been taught mainly in Buddhist centres and similar locales could now be made widely available for anyone to try.

While finishing my training in Bangor I had the great fortune to be introduced to John Teasdale, one of the founders of MBCT, who lives – as my wife and I do – in Cambridge. John and I took the mindfulness programme I'd been working with in Bangor, a hybrid of MBSR and MBCT, and tweaked it more particularly towards stress. We then spent some time teaching that programme, along with our colleague Ciaran Saunders, in public courses held in Cambridge. We made video recordings of each taught session and in between sessions the three of us would meet up, replay the recording of ourselves teaching, and comment on what we saw one another doing: what worked and what didn't work so well. That was one of the richest learning experiences of my whole engagement in the process of mindfulness teaching.

Soon after graduating I was invited to join the team of mindfulness teachers at the Centre for Mindfulness Research and Practice that is located in the School of Psychology at Bangor. I'm now an honorary lecturer there and for many years taught a module on the master's programme as well as co-leading mindfulness teacher-training retreats.

In 2006 I founded a mindfulness training company, Mindfulness Works Ltd, and with my associates I have since led many public courses in London and elsewhere based on what I learned at Bangor and developed with John.

But my interest in the world of work and business never went away and I've found myself increasingly drawn into that field. Part of this is because of what I keep finding on my public courses.

The sense I get from the public MBSR courses I lead is that, for a very large proportion of participants, the greatest source of stress and distress in their lives comes from what they encounter each day at work. I am convinced that, if we can train more mindful leaders, if we can help to create more mindful workplaces, we can have a huge impact on the overall levels of well-being in our society.

I wrote a book on this theme – *The Mindful Workplace* – and have come increasingly to teach in workplace and leadership contexts, as well as continuing with the public courses. More recently I have become an adjunct professor at IE Business School in Madrid, where I am honoured to be part of an extraordinary faculty teaching an executive master's in positive leadership and strategy (EXMPLS), which has mindfulness training at its heart. We draw in a high-powered student body from around the world and I'm deeply moved each time I meet the students to see the changes that their deepening engagement with mindfulness practice brings about.

BOX 4: THE EFFECTS OF MINDFULNESS TRAINING

It is because mindfulness works that it's being found in so many different contexts these days. The variety of approaches and applications is extraordinary. NICE, the UK's National Institute for Health and Clinical Excellence that advises the UK National Health Service on appropriate clinical provision, recommends it as a front-line treatment in instances of relapsing depression. The United States Marine Corps, on the other hand, has found that it helps soldiers remain mentally flexible, cognitively clear and emotionally appropriate under pressure. Some people use mindfulness to help them manage chronic pain and there is good research evidence for its efficacy there. Others come to it because they want to be more focused and effective at work, or because they want to be more resilient, or more empathic.

In whatever way or for whatever reason you come to mindfulness training, there is now a large body of evidence that shows that with just eight weeks of training really substantial changes are possible.

There is a considerable and growing body of research evidence around the effectiveness of mindfulness training these days. Peer-reviewed research papers are currently emerging at a rate of around 40 per month. I won't try to sum up all of that evidence here, but the UK's Mental Health Foundation commissioned a report which examined the health benefits of mindfulness training. Their 2010 *Mindfulness Report* noted that evidence coming from mindfulness and well-being research shows that mindfulness confers significant benefits on health, well-being and quality of life in general:

- According to the report, people who are more mindful are less likely to experience psychological distress, including depression and anxiety. They are less neurotic, more extroverted and report greater well-being and life satisfaction.
- They have greater awareness, understanding and acceptance of their emotions, and recover from bad moods more quickly.
- They have less frequent negative thoughts and are more able to let them go when they arise.
- They have higher, more stable self-esteem that is less dependent on external factors.
- They enjoy more satisfying relationships, are better at communicating and are less troubled by relationship conflict, as well as less likely to think negatively of their partners as a result of conflict.
- Mindfulness is correlated with emotional intelligence, which itself has been associated with good social skills, ability to cooperate and ability to see another person's perspective.
- People who are mindful are also less likely to react defensively or aggressively when they feel threatened. Mindfulness seems to increase self-awareness, and is associated with greater vitality.
- Being more mindful is linked with higher success in reaching academic and personal goals.
- Practising meditation has repeatedly been shown to improve people's attention, as well as improve job performance, productivity and satisfaction, and to enable better relationships with colleagues, resulting in a reduction of work-related stress.

- People who are mindful feel more in control of their behaviour and are more able to override or change internal thoughts and feelings and resist acting on impulse.
- Meditation practices more generally have been shown to increase blood flow, reduce blood pressure and protect people at risk of developing hypertension; they have also been shown to reduce the risk of developing and dying from cardiovascular disease, and to reduce the severity of cardiovascular disease when it does arise.
- People who meditate have fewer hospital admissions for heart disease, cancer and infectious diseases, and visit their doctor half as often as people who don't meditate.
- Mindfulness can reduce addictive behaviour, and meditation practices generally have been found to help reduce use of illegal drugs, prescribed medication, alcohol and caffeine.

Neuroscience Research

We also know that mindfulness training has a significant impact on how the brain is shaped, wired and activated. After just eight weeks of mindfulness training we know from separate studies that one might expect:

- increased brain grey-matter concentration in areas connected with sustained attention, emotional regulation and perspective taking;
- increased cortical thickness;
- decreased amygdala activation: the amygdala is a key component in the brain's threat-detection system – when it is less active you feel more at ease with yourself and others;
- increased activity in the left prefrontal cortex and less activity in the right prefrontal cortex: the ratio of left to right

prefrontal activation is a good predictor of overall happiness and well-being – if the left prefrontal is more active then you're likely to experience higher levels of well-being;

- increased working-memory capacity: working memory is the system that actively holds information in the mind to do tasks such as reasoning and comprehension, and to make it available for further information processing. Measures of working-memory capacity are strongly related to success in the performance of complex cognitive tasks. It is also a key component in emotion regulation and it is reduced by acute or chronic stress.

The skills that emerge from mindfulness training are gradually beginning to be recognised as crucial life skills. Really, we should all have learned them at school and it is deeply heartening that programmes for schoolchildren and young adults, like .b and the programme developed by my colleagues at Bangor University, are beginning to find their way into schools. Most of us missed that chance, but thankfully it is never too late to learn.

I sometimes begin my programmes by asking how many people in the room think that regular physical training can be crucial for their health and well-being. Everyone puts up their hand. I then ask how many people think that regular mental training can be crucial for their health and well-being. Most people put up their hand, a little more tentatively perhaps. I then point out that, had I asked the physical-training question to a general audience at the end of the nineteenth century, very few would have raised their hand. And, indeed, even as late as 1970, when the New York City marathon was first run with 127 entrants, of whom fewer than half completed the course, it was thought that only a few thousand people in the United States had the capacity to run a marathon. In 2010, 44,829 people finished – a world record for a marathon race –

and every year tens of thousands of potential entrants are un-successful in the lottery for starting places.

There has been a paradigm shift in our cultural attitude to physical fitness.

We are now on the brink of another paradigm shift. We are beginning to recognise the importance of what we might think of as mental and emotional fitness and to see how we can train to build this.

When you're more skilled at working with your mind and mental states, things go better: for you and everyone around you.

Before Beginning the Course

You will read about a number of different mindfulness practices in each chapter of this book. If you're using the book as a do-it-yourself manual for the eight-week course, it would be best to do the practices in the order in which they are described.

To that end, it would be good, if you can, to read the book at a time when and in a place where you're less likely to be disturbed. It would also be good to be able to engage in some of the meditations in the order in which they are taught. Some of the time, where indicated, you might want to put the book aside and take the time to listen to the particular audio material for that part of the course. The track name and its timing are shown at the appropriate place in the text.

Since you'll be doing different meditations from time to time, it will generally be good to have access to an upright chair, rather like a kitchen or dining chair, or a meditation bench or cushion if you want to meditate sitting on the floor. I'll say more about the postures for sitting meditation when we come to that part of the course.

For Week One, beginning in the following chapter, there are two other items of equipment you'll need.

There is the option for doing one of our meditations lying on the floor, so you might want to have a rug or mat handy for that.

And our first meditation is going to be an eating meditation. But we're not going to eat very much – just one raisin in fact – and I'll be providing fairly detailed guidance on how to do that as an eating meditation. So if you're going to read on, now might be a good time to go and find yourself a raisin. If you don't have one handy, a very small section of any fruit or vegetable that you can eat will do instead.

WEEK

ONE

AUTOMATIC PILOT

We're going to begin this week with the eating meditation I talked about in the Introduction. By eating just one small raisin, mindfully, I hope you'll get a deeper sense of some of what mindfulness is all about. So have your raisin or your small section of a fruit or vegetable handy and get ready to play 'The Raisin Exercise' (⬇1 ⏱15mins) on your audio player.

If you don't want to listen to the exercise right now, you could read about it instead in Box 1.

If you're going to listen to the audio, get yourself into an upright and alert but relaxed posture, let the raisin or whatever you're using instead rest on one of your open palms and play the audio now.

BOX 1: THE RAISIN EXERCISE

Get hold of a single raisin and find somewhere quiet where you can sit for 10 or 15 minutes and give your full attention to this exercise.

1. HOLDING
- Let the raisin rest in your palm. Take a few moments to become aware of its weight.
- Then become aware of its temperature – any warmth or coolness it may have.

2. LOOKING

- Give the raisin your full attention, really looking.
- Become aware of the pattern of colour and shape that the raisin makes as it rests on your palm – almost like an abstract painting.

3. TOUCHING

- As best you can, being aware of the sense of movement in your muscles as you do this, pick up the raisin between the thumb and forefinger of your other hand.
- Explore the outside texture of the raisin as you roll it very gently between the thumb and forefinger.
- Squeeze it ever so slightly and notice that this might give you a sense of its interior texture.
- Notice perhaps that you can feel this difference just with your thumb and forefinger – the interior texture and the exterior texture.

4. SEEING

- Lift the raisin to a place where you can really focus on it and begin to examine it in even greater detail.
- Notice highlights and shadows. See how these change as it moves in the light.
- Notice how facets of it appear and disappear – how it may seem to have ridges and valleys and how these may shift and change.

5. SMELLING

- Again aware of the sense of movement in your muscles, begin to move the raisin very slowly towards your mouth.
- As it passes by your nose you may become aware of its fragrance. With each inhalation, really explore that fragrance.

- Become aware of any changes that may be taking place now in your mouth or stomach – any salivation, perhaps.

6. PLACING

- Bring the raisin up to your lips. Explore the delicate sensation of touch here.
- Now place it in your mouth but don't chew.
- Just let it rest on your tongue, noticing any very faint flavour that may be there –
- or maybe not.
- Feel the contact it makes with the roof of the mouth, perhaps.
- Now move it to between your back teeth and just let it rest there – again without chewing.
- Notice any urges or impulses in the body.

7. TASTING

- Now take a single bite. Just one. Notice any flavour.
- Then take another bite. Notice any change in flavour.
- Then another bite, and another.

8. CHEWING

- Now slowly, very slowly, chew.
- Be aware of sound, of texture, of flavour and of change.
- Keep chewing in this way, very slowly, until there is almost nothing left to chew.

9. SWALLOWING

- When there is almost nothing left to chew, swallow. See if you can be aware of the intention to swallow as it first arises.

10. FINISHING

- Follow what is left of the raisin as it moves down towards your stomach and you lose sight of it altogether.

How does your body feel now as you've completed that exercise?

What did you notice that you might not have been aware of before?

There's no telling what you will find when you do this exercise. We're all different and we all come to the process with our own unique histories and ways of seeing. What's really important here is that you allow your experience of doing that exercise simply to be what it was – there is no right or wrong way of doing it. What's really key is that you notice and reflect on what you actually experienced. What was it like, in detail, for you?

You might want to spend a few moments now turning the experience over in your mind. What did you notice as you went through the exercise? If nothing much comes to mind, here are some things you might want to consider:

- What struck you most about the exercise?
- How did the raisin feel on your palm?
- What did you notice as you examined its colour and shape?
- What did you notice when you explored it with your fingers?
- And when you looked at it more closely?
- Was there any aroma? What was that like?
- How did it feel in your mouth?
- Were you aware of any impulses as the raisin sat between your back teeth *before* you began to bite and chew?
- If there were, what was it like to sit with an impulse and not act on it?

- What was the first bite like?
- And the second?
- How did it sound as you chewed?
- How did it taste?
- What did it feel like, eating a raisin so slowly?
- Anything else?

This isn't an exercise in trying to *remember* the details of the exercise. It's more about just noticing what you noticed.

Some people find the experience deeply enjoyable. 'I never knew what a raisin tasted like before!' Others find it unpleasant: 'I thought I enjoyed raisins, but actually I discovered that I really hate the taste of them – the skin was really bitter. I just never noticed that before.' Sometimes people say the opposite: 'I don't like raisins, and I wasn't looking forward to this at all, but that wasn't bad at all. In fact I quite liked it.' Some people comment on the shape, or the touch, or the colour, or how the smell evokes early memories. Some people find that their mind just keeps wandering off to think of other things – maybe things sparked off by elements of the experience. Some people find that they don't experience very much at all.

We have such different experiences – some pleasant, some unpleasant. But whether it's pleasant or unpleasant, whether there's a lot of experience or very little, whether you stayed focused on the experience or your mind kept wandering off is neither here nor there in this context. This exercise is just about *noticing* what you experienced.

Most of the time, when we eat a raisin we do it on a kind of automatic pilot. We can eat raisins by the handful even – while we're also watching television, or getting the kids ready for school, or driving, or having a conversation and so on – and we don't notice what they feel like in our hands, what they look like, smell like or taste like.

We miss these things, but we get by. As humans, we've got this extraordinary capacity to do sometimes even quite complex things on automatic pilot, without needing to notice what we're doing much.

Have you ever driven 30 miles down the road and then suddenly asked yourself 'How did I get here?' Most drivers have had that experience. Sometimes it's as if we're driving completely on automatic pilot. That really is extraordinary because, when you think about it, driving a car is a potentially lethal activity. If you are driving on a motorway, in the central lane say, at 70 miles per hour, there might be huge trucks thundering along on the inside lane at 60 miles per hour and powerful cars hurling past in the outside lane at 80 to 100 miles per hour. One twitch of the steering wheel in either direction and you'd maybe die and certainly cause mayhem. Yet you can do it completely automatically, all the time thinking, planning, dreaming or imagining – barely showing up for the journey. We do this, and we don't find complete carnage on our motorways. Human beings are really good at automatic pilot.

When you first began to drive a car you couldn't do that. At first, it's all very clunky and you certainly can't do much thinking about a complex piece of work that you have to get ready for next week when you're still trying to figure out, in real time, which of those pedals is the clutch and which the brake. You probably couldn't even have had a light conversation while you were first trying to do that. But in time you automate all of the driving routines and off you go. You can now drive more or less automatically and your mental resources are freed up for other things.

Automatic pilot extends your capacity by creating habits and habitual behaviours that take fewer brain resources than conscious ones do – and this is a wonderful capacity. We get through our days by running a huge series of automatic routines.

For example, like most people, my wife and I have our 'turning in for the night' automatic routine. At some time, usually between 10.30 p.m. and 11.30 p.m., we decide it's time to turn in and off we go – turn off the television, turn off the heating, check the back door is locked, check the cat is in, lock the front door, up the stairs, brush teeth . . . and so on.

We don't give it a thought. We don't suddenly go 'Oh my gosh! It's time to go to bed. What shall we do? Where to start? I know – the back door. You check the back door and I'll . . . I'll check the front door. Right. Done. Now what? Oh yes, the television. I'll do the television – you do the heating. Great! Done. Now . . . Cat. Where's the cat . . .?'

None of that. We just run our normal turning in for the night routine, and we have hundreds, maybe thousands of these that get us through the day.

That's great, but there are a few problems.

ON AUTOMATIC PILOT WE MISS THINGS

When you're on automatic pilot you can miss things. Some of what you miss can really enrich your life. Those few moments between your home and the train station in the morning, when you might have tuned in to the quality of the light or a sense of welcome freshness in the air. But you missed it because you were running your 'thinking about my to-do list' routine on automatic pilot – maybe already for the tenth time that morning.

In ways like this you miss so much that can enrich your life and in simple ways enhance the quality of your days – and your life. The first few buds in spring, a cobweb catching the light, the sound of a bird, the taste of a melon. They take hardly any time, but when you miss such things your life is just a tiny bit impoverished – and these things add up. When you catch them, in simple and easy ways your life gets richer and richer.

Some of what you miss can be really important. That look in a child's eye in the morning that might have told her mum that she was being bullied at school and didn't want to go. But her mum missed it because she was just running her familiar 'family breakfast' routine on automatic pilot and not paying attention. Or that tone of voice in a colleague's greeting in the morning that says he's got real problems at home that he really needs to talk about as they're affecting his work. But you miss it because you're just doing your 'arriving at work' routine on automatic pilot.

So, although the capacity to do things on automatic pilot is really important and valuable, it's also sometimes really important to come out of automatic pilot – to consciously show up for your life. A life lived mainly on automatic pilot is poorer and less effective than it might be. In some ways it's barely a life at all.

And there are other issues as well.

OUR AUTOMATIC-PILOT SYSTEM CAN BECOME OVERLOADED

Running an automatic-pilot routine can be like opening a new window in a computer. That can be an efficient way of getting things done. But sometimes you can have too many windows open, too many routines running, and then the computer starts to slow and may even eventually crash. There's just too much going on, too many conflicting routines running.

At work, for example, you begin to feel overwhelmed as yet another email pings into your inbox, while you're speaking to a colleague who dropped in with an urgent request, as you were trying to work out what to do about that piece of work from last week that ran over deadline and wondering how your partner would take it if you cancelled yet another evening at home together . . .

Sometimes you need to consciously come out of automatic pilot and choose to focus – but in a particular way.

At such times, it can be unhelpful to try to *think* your way out of the problem. That would be like opening yet another window on a computer that's already running slowly and may be about to crash. Instead, you need to shut down some of the windows and allow your mental and emotional resources to engage with just one thing.

Mindfulness training helps you to spot when you're overloaded before things start going wrong. It helps you to come away from automatic routines and focus more effectively on each simple passing moment.

SOME OF OUR AUTOMATIC ROUTINES CAN BE REALLY UNHELPFUL

In Box 2 of the Introduction, 'Mindfulness-Based Cognitive Therapy' (*see page 15*), I talked about Mary, who came home tired from work to an answerphone message from her partner saying he was going to be home late that evening. That sparked a cascade of automatic-pilot routines in Mary, which led to her low mood very rapidly escalating into depression. Whether things happen in quite that sort of way for you or not, the underlying propensity at work here is universal. We all find that one way or another we can run mental and emotional automatic-pilot routines that feed off one another in unhelpful ways and don't serve us very well at all.

Some of us run an 'I'm not good enough' automatic routine. Whatever we try to do there's a quiet inner voice in the background commenting on how we don't quite measure up. Or we may run the opposite, an 'I'm really great' automatic routine, constantly evaluating ourselves against others, putting them down and trying to boost ourselves along. Or there are 'catastrophising' routines, where we always imagine a worst-case outcome. There is a really vast range of these unhelpful automatic routines, or cognitive distortions, that we can run and I've listed some of these in Box 2.

BOX 2: UNHELPFUL AUTOMATIC ROUTINES

Here is a list of mental habits we can have that really don't serve us very well. See if any of these ring a bell for you.

ALL-OR-NOTHING THINKING. Here, you see things in black and white as opposed to shades of grey. 'Things *never* go well for me!' Or, if a waiter fumbles your order in a restaurant: 'This place is rubbish – our evening is ruined!' Or if someone you admire makes a minor mistake, your admiration quickly turns to contempt.

OVERGENERALISATION. This involves making rapid generalisations from insufficient experience or evidence. A lonely person spends most of her time at home. Friends sometimes invite her to dinner so she can meet new people. 'There's no point in that,' she thinks. 'No one would like me.'

FILTERING. We all have a tendency to filter out information that doesn't conform to our already held beliefs. Often, this involves focusing entirely on negative elements of a situation to the exclusion of the positive. For example, you've just given a presentation to 20 people at work. Everyone says how useful they found it. As they're leaving, one colleague mentions a small point where she thinks there may have been some confusion. Immediately you

come to think that the presentation was dreadful and you
didn't do well enough.

DISQUALIFYING THE POSITIVE. On being congratulated
about having done something really well, you put half of
the congratulation down to flattery, and say – whether out
of modesty or out of doubt – 'Well, it wasn't that good,
really.'

MIND READING. Here, you infer someone's probable,
usually negative, thoughts from their behaviour and non-
verbal communication. 'I know he doesn't like me from the
way he turned just then.' Or you take precautions against
the worst suspected case without investigating further.
'I know writing up my thoughts for her as she asked is
going to be a waste of time – she's already made up
her mind.'

FORTUNE TELLING. This involves predicting, usually
negatively, the outcome of events which might turn out
quite differently. Despite being very well prepared for your
exam you think: 'I just know I'm going to fail.'

MAGNIFICATION AND MINIMISATION. Here, you give
more weight to a perceived failure, weakness or threat and
less weight to a perceived success, strength or opportunity.
Or the other way around.

CATASTROPHISING. This involves giving undue weight to
the worst possible outcome, however unlikely. 'I just know
this is going to be a disaster!' It also involves experiencing
a situation as unbearable or impossible when it is just
uncomfortable.

EMOTIONAL REASONING. Here, you presume that any
negative feelings you may have actually expose the true
nature of things or you think something is true based solely
on a feeling. 'I feel I'm stupid or boring – therefore I must
be.' Or feeling that your fear of flying in planes actually

means that planes are a very dangerous way to travel.

'SHOULD' STATEMENTS. This involves expecting yourself and others always and without exception to do what you morally should do, irrespective of the particular situation. For example, after a performance, a concert pianist believes he or she *should not* have made so many mistakes. Or, while waiting for an appointment, you think that your dentist *should* be on time, and feel bitter and resentful as a result, without considering any possible emergency they may be having to deal with.

LABELLING. This involves attributing someone's actions to their character instead of to some accidental attribute. Instead of just thinking that you made a mistake, you think 'I'm a loser' because only a loser would make that kind of mistake. Or someone who makes a bad first impression is simply 'a jerk' and they're written off without further evidence of their character.

MISLABELLING. This involves describing something with language that has a strong and often unconscious connotation of other values. So someone who really values the bond between a mother and child speaks of a woman who puts her children in a nursery as 'abandoning her children to strangers'.

PERSONALISATION. Here, you take personal responsibility, including any praise or blame, for events over which you have no actual control. For instance, a mother whose child is struggling in school automatically blames herself for being a bad mother when, in fact, the real cause of her child's perceived failure might have been something else entirely.

BLAMING. This involves holding other people exclusively responsible for your own distress. For example, a spouse may blame their husband or wife entirely for their marital problems, instead of looking at his or her own part in the situation.

ALWAYS BEING RIGHT. Here, you always imagine that whatever goes wrong in any situation must be the fault of others.

ON AUTOMATIC PILOT IT'S EASY TO HAVE YOUR BUTTONS PRESSED

We all have our triggers – events that happen in the world, things other people might say to us, memories or patterns of thinking that spark off one or another reactive cycle. A wife jokingly says to her husband, 'Oh, you're such a slob!' and in seconds he's gone back to being an unhappy thirteen-year-old, collapsed in on himself and struggling to re-engage. An old, established pattern of thinking, feeling, sensing and impulses kicks in, as if out of nowhere, and down he goes.

When you're aware of your thoughts, feelings, sensations and impulses from moment to moment, that can open up much more freedom. You may begin to find that you don't any longer have to go down the old familiar mental ruts that caused you difficulties in the past.

MINDFULNESS TRAINING OPENS UP CHOICE

Although there's nothing wrong with automatic routines as such, some of them can be really unhelpful. With a bit of training in mindfulness, it becomes easier to spot unhelpful automatic routines for what they are. You can learn to see when you're in danger of becoming overwhelmed and you can learn how to step out of automatic pilot at such times. You can learn how to take moments in each day to come away from automatic pilot and drop into mindful awareness. That can be powerfully renewing and enriching.

You can begin to notice some of the inner unhelpful automatic-pilot routines that you run. You might catch yourself ruminating, or catastrophising, or being unduly self-critical or whatever your particular predisposition may be. You may then begin to learn the art of recognising such thoughts simply as thoughts and to treat yourself and all your patterns and habits with warmth and kindness.

When you notice what you're doing in your mind at such times it begins to be easier to switch your attention to somewhere else. After all, if there was that much to experience in a single raisin, what else might there be to explore and mindfully engage with?

Please note, though: mindfulness isn't about doing things slowly. It's about doing them with full attention. Novak Djokovic, one of the world's most formidable tennis players, uses yoga and meditation to keep himself in good physical, mental and emotional shape – and he's one of the fastest guys on the court!

THE BODY-SCAN MEDITATION

Our next meditation is the body scan. I've provided two versions of this as audio files. There's a longer version that takes around 35 minutes to complete and a shorter version of 15 minutes. The version you use for home practice will depend on which home-practice stream you're undertaking. It would be good, though, the first time you do the practice, to try the longer version – at least once. You may, in fact, try to do that right now. If you have 35 to 40 minutes to spare and you're not going to be disturbed, you could choose to do the body-scan practice.

The instructions we'll be working with now are on the track entitled 'The Body Scan (Longer Version)' (⬇2 ⏱35 mins). If you don't want to do the practice at this moment, when I give the instruction to play the audio you could instead just scan Box 3 briefly to get a sense of what the practice is like.

In the body scan, you bring mindful attention to each of the different parts of your body in turn. The intention of the practice is to be awake and aware. It isn't intended to help you be more relaxed or calm. That may happen, or it may not. Rather, the aim of the practice is to become more aware, directly sensing whatever bodily sensations (or lack of them) you find in each moment as you focus your attention on different parts of the body in turn.

Before doing the body scan, try this very brief exercise, right now, for a few moments.

- Begin by looking at your hands for a few moments.
- Now, spend a few moments *thinking* about your hands. Just let your thoughts go wherever they take you while you're thinking about your hands.
- Now, put the book to one side and clap your hands together twice – quite forcefully.
- Now, *feel* what is going on in your hands. What sensations do you find? Tingling? Stinging? Warmth . . .?

Notice the difference here between *thinking* about your hands and *feeling* your hands. It is the latter that you're going to focus on in the body scan – your actual body sensations, in each changing moment.

In the exercise above, I first of all asked you to create a fairly obvious sensation in your hands that you could pay attention to. Most of us don't find that extent of sensation in every part of our bodies when we do the body scan. That's fine. The aim of the practice is simply to feel whatever sensations you actually feel, from moment to moment, even if it's not very much at all. You might even find that there are parts of the body where it seems there is almost no sensation at all. That's fine, it's perfectly normal and the intention is just to notice whatever is there.

You can do the body scan either lying down on a mat or a rug on the floor or on your bed. You can also do it sitting upright in a chair. Many of us today suffer from some degree of sleep deprivation, and when you do the body scan it can be very easy to fall asleep. Although that might be refreshing, it's not the intention of the practice. Instead, the intention is to remain as awake and as aware as you can be. If you *do* fall asleep for a few moments you can always just pick the practice up again. If sleepiness becomes a problem, you might find it helps to prop your head up with a pillow, to open your eyes, or to do the practice sitting up rather than lying down.

So decide how you want to do the practice now – lying down or sitting up – and when you're ready, play the audio file 'The Body Scan (Longer Version)' (⊙2 ⊙35 mins) or scan through the instructions in Box 3.

 ## BOX 3: THE BODY SCAN

Settling
To begin with, take whatever time you need to settle into the posture you have chosen for the practice. If you're doing this lying down, perhaps lying in a fairly symmetrical posture, with your legs uncrossed and your arms by your side. Prop your head up with a small pillow or cushion if you need to. Make sure you're warm or cool enough and that you won't be disturbed.

Focusing on the Breath

When you're ready, begin to become aware of the movement of your breath and the sensations in your body. In particular, perhaps, start by becoming aware of the sensations in your belly, feeling the changing patterns of sensation there as you breathe in and out. Take a few minutes to really feel and explore those sensations. Then, become aware of any sense of touch and pressure where your body meets whatever you're lying or sitting on. Now, you might try taking a few more deliberate out-breaths and in-breaths, maybe placing a hand on your belly to help you track the breath. With each out-breath, let yourself settle more fully into the floor or bed or chair. After a few such breaths, when you're settled, move your hand away from your belly and just allow the breath to come and go as it does.

Scanning the Body

When you're ready, begin to explore the changing physical sensations in your body, right now. Start by bringing the spotlight of your awareness to the big toe of your left foot. What sensations do you find there right now? Warmth, coolness, tingling, tickling? Nothing much at all? Just notice whatever's there. As much as you can, bring a warm and kindly curiosity to whatever you find. Then, move that focus to each of the toes in turn, bringing a gentle, interested, affectionate attention to what you find, perhaps noticing the sense of contact between the toes, a sense of tingling, warmth, perhaps numbness – whatever's there.

Then, when you are ready, on an in-breath, feel or imagine the breath entering the lungs, and passing all the way down the body, down the left leg, all the way to the toes of the left foot. And, on the out-breath, feel or imagine the breath coming all the way back up from the toes, to the foot, right up the leg and torso and out through the nose. Continue breathing in this way for a few breaths, breathing down to the toes on each in-breath, and back out from the toes on each out-breath. Practise this 'breathing into' as best you can, approaching it playfully, imaginatively, experimentally.

When you're ready, on an out-breath, let go of attention to the toes, and bring your attention to the sensations on the bottom of your left foot – bringing a gentle, investigative curiosity to sensations at the sole of the foot, the instep, the heel (noticing, perhaps, the sensations where the heel makes contact with the floor or mat or bed). Experiment with 'breathing with' any and all sensations – being aware of the breath in the background, as, in the foreground, you explore the sensations in the bottom of the foot.

Now allow the spotlight of attention to broaden into the rest of the foot – to the ankle, the top of the foot, the whole of the foot. Then, when you're ready, on an out-breath, let go of attention to the left foot completely and let the focus of attention move into the lower left leg – the calf, shin, knee, in turn.

Continue to scan the body in this way, lingering for a time on each part of the body in turn: the left shin, the left knee, the left thigh; the right toes and then foot and ankle, the right lower leg, the right knee, the right thigh; the pelvic area – groin, genitals, buttocks and hips; the lower back and the abdomen, the upper back, the ribs and the chest.

Then move to the hands, doing both at the same time. Begin by exploring the sensations at the tips of the fingers and thumbs. For a few breaths, direct the breath to the finger and thumb tips, breathing down to the finger and thumb tips on the in-breath, up from them on the out-breath, then expanding the attention to all parts of the fingers and thumbs. And from there to the palms and the backs of both hands, the wrists, the lower arms and elbows, the upper arms, the shoulders, the neck, the face (jaw, mouth, lips, nose, cheeks, ears, eyes, forehead) and then the entire head.

Finally, bring attention to the crown of the head. You might feel or imagine that there's a hole there, rather like the blowhole of a whale, and you can breathe in and breathe out through that. Breathing in through the crown of the head, direct the breath down the body and sweep the body with the breath, maybe breathing out through the soles of the feet. And, perhaps breathing in through the feet, sweep the breath up through the body and out through the head.

In whatever way works for you now, try sweeping the body with the breath for a few breaths as you begin to bring the practice to a close. Spend a few minutes being aware of a sense of the body as a whole, and of the breath flowing freely in and out of the body before mindfully beginning to move again.

While doing the body scan, if you become aware of tension or other intense sensations in a part of the body, you might try 'breathing into' that sensation, using the in-breath gently to carry your awareness right into the sensation, bringing some warmth and kindness there. Maybe the tension will release, maybe it won't. And if it doesn't, just see what it's like to be with it, letting it be. As best you can, bring an attitude of warmth and kindness to yourself and your body.

If, after a while, you begin to feel uncomfortable and

you want to move, you have a choice. You could mindfully move – being aware of the intention to move and all of the sensations that come with the movement. Or you might see what it's like just to sit with whatever sensations are there – letting them be, bringing an attitude of warm, kindly curiosity to what's there.

The mind will inevitably wander away from the breath and the body from time to time. That's perfectly normal, it's what minds do. When you notice that the mind has wandered, just acknowledge that, seeing where the attention went off to, and then gently returning it to the part of the body you intended to focus on. If it helps, you might silently say to yourself, 'Ah, there's thinking . . .' or 'there's planning . . .' or 'dreaming . . .' – whatever it is, and then gently, kindly, return the attention to the body.

AFTER THE BODY SCAN

Here are some of the sorts of things that mindfulness-course participants sometimes report after they have done the body scan for the first time:

> I had hardly any sensation in my toes. I could feel some sensation as we moved up the legs, but I hardly felt anything at all in my lower legs. That was really strange and uncomfortable because I thought I ought to be feeling something there.

It can be quite strange at first to see how your bodily sensations actually present themselves. In some parts of the body you might feel a lot, in some parts hardly anything at all. That's not right, it's not wrong – it's just how you find it. Notice how we quickly move to judgement here. We're set up to think that there's a right way of doing this, and we want to do it right – we want to feel sensations wherever the guidance takes us. If we don't we can feel we're not doing it right or it's not the way it should be.

Perhaps just notice that tendency to judge. You could even say to yourself, in a friendly kind of way: 'Oh yes, there I go, judging my experience again . . .' and then come back to what you're actually experiencing.

I just kept falling asleep . . .

This is not at all uncommon. Many of us in our culture are a little sleep-deprived. It's not a problem to fall asleep for a few minutes. It might even be quite refreshing and if it happens you can just carry on with wherever the instruction has got to when you wake up again.

If you find you keep falling asleep and you're missing large parts of the practice, and you want to stay awake, you might do the practice sitting upright in a chair, or with your eyes open. Just experiment and see what works best for you.

I felt so fidgety. It was really uncomfortable. I just wanted to move around. But I was gritting my teeth and hanging on – really resisting that urge to move.

Notice what's going on here. It's easy to fall into a kind of striving attitude, trying to 'do it right'. Maybe see what it's like for a few moments just to acknowledge 'Oh yes, there's restlessness . . .' Or whatever. And then, if you keep wanting to move, just mindfully move. Or you might try staying with it for a bit longer, exploring your experience in each moment.

There's no right way or wrong way of handling that. Just experiment and see what you find.

But I thought this was supposed to help me relax!

Of course many of us would love to relax a bit more, and the body scan may help you to relax or it may not. But that's not the main thing here. The aim of the exercise is to enable you to be more mindful and to discover what goes on for you in each moment and to bring a kindly awareness to that.

> I kept finding itches in different parts of my body and I really wanted to scratch. At one point I just opened my eyes to see what time it was but then I thought, 'Oh, I'm not supposed to do that.'

Itches can be really uncomfortable, of course. But maybe there's another way of being with an experience like that. With an itch, you might even see if you can allow it to be there and explore it. Where is it most intense? Where is it least intense? Is it changing . . . moving . . . pulsing . . .? Can you open to it and explore it? In the end, there's no problem with gently and mindfully scratching. Just as there's no problem with opening your eyes for a few moments. There's no right way, no wrong way, to do this exercise. There's just what you find, what you mindfully experience. That's the main thing.

> My mind kept wandering.

That's what minds do. When your mind wanders, just notice where it went and gently bring it back. You could say to yourself: 'Oh yes, there I was planning again . . .' and then gently and kindly bring your mind back. And if it wanders a hundred times, just bring it back a hundred times. It's all great practice.

With the body scan, you begin to make a deeper acquaintance with your own body. Like Mister Duffy in James Joyce's *The Dubliners* who 'lived a little distance from his body', many of us in the twenty-first century can be a bit divorced from our bodies. We spend so much of our time taking in information from electronic media (computers, tablets, phones, emails and so on) that we can, if we're not careful, become more like balloons on sticks than fully embodied human beings. We can begin to treat our bodies as if their mere purpose is to carry our minds about. But that attitude misses the point entirely. To experience the full breadth of our humanity we need to wake up to the whole body–mind system, and that involves extending our experience beyond just 'thinking about' things.

BOX 4: IF I HAD MY LIFE TO LIVE OVER

When you're mindful, you live more fully. The following lines, so far as I can tell, began life in a piece authored by the American humourist and cartoonist Don Herold. Published by the *Reader's Digest* in October 1953 under the title 'I'd Pick More Daisies', they then went through a variety of changes – a version of them eventually being translated into Spanish and attributed to the Argentinian writer Jorge Luis Borges. They were then retranslated into English as a poem by Borges. I first encountered them in a handbook of mindfulness instruction, in which they were attributed to 'Nadine Stair – aged 85'.

Both the lines themselves and the story of their constant transmutation have something to tell us about mindfulness. When you really look, it turns out that there's more going on than you first thought.

If I Had My Life to Live Over

I'd like to make more mistakes next time.

I'd relax, I would limber up. I would be sillier than I have been on this trip. I would take fewer things seriously. I would take more chances. I would climb more mountains and swim more rivers. I would eat more ice cream and less beans. I would perhaps have more actual troubles, but I'd have fewer imaginary ones.

You see, I'm one of those people who live sensibly and sanely hour after hour, day after day. Oh, I've had my moments, and if I had to do it over again I'd have more of them. In fact, I'd try to have nothing else. Just moments, one after another, instead of living so many years ahead of each day. I've been one of those persons who never goes anywhere without a thermometer, a hot water bottle, a raincoat, and a parachute. If I had to do it again, I would travel lighter than I have.

If I had my life to live over, I would start barefoot earlier in the spring and stay that way later in the fall. I would go to more dances. I would ride more merrygorounds. I would pick more daisies.

BOX 5: TIPS FOR THE BODY SCAN

- Regardless of what you find when you do the practice, just do it! If you fall asleep, lose concentration, keep thinking of other things, find yourself focusing over and again on the 'wrong' part of the body, don't feel anything . . . these are your experiences in the moment. As best you can, simply be aware of them – with kindness and curiosity.
- If your mind wanders a lot, just note the thoughts as passing events and gently bring the mind back to the body scan – over and over and over.
- See if it's possible to let go of ideas of success or failure, or of 'doing it really well'. This isn't a competition and it's not a skill you need to strive for. The only discipline involved is regular and frequent practice. Just do it with an open and kindly attitude.
- Try letting go of any expectations about what the body

scan will do for you. Maybe imagine it as a seed you've planted. The more you poke around and interfere, the less it will be able to develop. Just give the body scan the right conditions – relative peace and quiet, regular and frequent practice – that's enough. The more you try deliberately to bring about any specific outcomes, the more that conscious effort will actually interfere with the seed's capacity to emerge.

- See what it's like to approach your experience in each moment with the attitude: 'OK, that's just the way things are right now.' Try letting what is the case be the case, with an attitude of kindness. If you try to fight off unpleasant thoughts, feelings or body sensations, that will only distract you from doing anything else.
- Above all, just do it.

BOX 6: STREAM 1
HOME PRACTICE FOR WEEK ONE

- Practise the body-scan meditation for at least six days of the coming week. Use 'The Body Scan (Longer Version)' (⊙2 ⊕35 mins) for guidance. Don't expect to feel anything in particular from doing the practice, rather – as much as possible – put aside all expectations about it. Just let your experience be your experience.
- If you would like to, maybe start a journal where you can make a brief note of the experiences that emerge for you each time you do the practice.
- Choose a routine activity in your daily life and make a deliberate effort to bring moment-to-moment awareness to that activity each time you do it, just as we did in the raisin exercise. Possibilities include things like your first cup of tea

or coffee, brushing your teeth, showering, drying yourself or getting dressed; your walk to the bus, train or car; eating – anything that you do every day. Just make a point of knowing what you are doing as you are actually doing it.

- Note any times when you find yourself able to become more deeply aware of what you eat in the same way you noticed the raisin. Eat at least one meal mindfully (and that doesn't necessarily mean slowly) – in the way that you ate the raisin.

BOX 7: STREAM 2
HOME PRACTICE FOR WEEK ONE

- Practise the body-scan meditation for at least six days of the coming week. Use 'The Body Scan (Shorter Version)' (⊙3 ⊙15 mins) for guidance. Don't expect to feel anything in particular from doing the practice, rather – as much as possible – put aside all expectations about it. Just let your experience be your experience.
- If you would like to, maybe start a journal where you can make a brief note of the experiences that emerge for you each time you do the practice.
- Choose a routine activity in your daily life and make a deliberate effort to bring moment-to-moment awareness to that activity each time you do it, just as we did in the raisin exercise. Possibilities include things like your first cup of tea or coffee, brushing your teeth, showering, drying yourself or getting dressed; your walk to the bus, train or car; eating – anything that you do every day. Just make a point of knowing what you are doing as you are actually doing it.

- Note any times when you find yourself able to become more deeply aware of what you eat in the same way you noticed the raisin. Eat at least one meal mindfully (and that doesn't necessarily mean slowly) – in the way that you ate the raisin.

WEEK

TWO

MINDFULNESS OF THE BREATH

This week introduces the first of the sitting meditations you'll be doing on this course, beginning with a meditation that focuses on the breath.

The breath is always there. You can't leave home without it, and so long as you're breathing there's a great deal more that is right with you than there is wrong with you.

To breathe is to be alive. Every single moment of your life is connected to the next by a breath, from the first one you took as you were born to the last you'll take when you die – one breath after another. Each of these breaths is unique, each one is different. The breath is constantly changing, shaped by your moods, bodily states and activity, and there is a two-way relationship between your breath and your emotions. You breathe short and shallow when you're tense or angry, erratically when you're upset, fast when you're excited, slow and deep when you're happy or contented, and you almost stop breathing when you're afraid.

Your emotions change the way you breathe, and the way you breathe can also change your emotions. Imagine you find yourself breathing quite short breaths. When you notice that, you come to realise that you're tense, so you pause – take a few more deliberate and slow in-breaths and out-breaths – and that helps you to become somewhat calmer. At other times you might use the breath to prepare for a challenge: you take a deeper in-breath, hold it for a beat or two . . . and off you go.

When you're tuned into it, the breath can be an emotional barometer – helping you to read the quality of your inner weather; and it can help you to regulate your emotions – to calm down when you need to, or to get ready for a difficult task, for example.

Many of the practices you'll be doing on this course begin by tuning in to the breath. Over time, you may begin to notice more easily how it changes in relation to your moods, emotions, thoughts and activity. This isn't about controlling the breath. Rather, it's about being more aware of it, more interested in what it's up to, there in the background.

That awareness can then help you to relax tensions when you need to or to focus more sharply when that's called for. Your awareness of the breath can come to be like an anchor – a steadying point to come back to in times of need.

That said, it's important to acknowledge that this isn't the case for everyone. There are people who have breathing difficulties, such as asthma for example, and there are those whose relationship to the breath in various ways can be more complex. If that is what goes on for you, you could perhaps begin by seeing what it's like to come along on this journey at least for a few steps. Might your relationship to the breath begin to change as we move through the course? If you don't want to do that, when I refer to the breath as we go along you may prefer to choose another focus for yourself – your heartbeat, for example, or the sensations in your hands or feet. Experiment and see what works best for you.

The first sitting meditation on the course is called the 'mindfulness of breathing' meditation. Here, you settle into a comfortable meditation posture, such as one of those described in Box 1, and then – after a short period of calming and tuning in to the body – you allow your attention to settle on the breath. On each in-breath and each out-breath.

As you'll have noticed with the body scan, minds wander – it's just what they do – so each time you become aware that your mind has wandered away from the breath you simply notice where it went to and then gently and kindly return your attention to the breath.

See what it's like here to cultivate a warm and friendly interest in the quality of each breath. Each breath is unique, and so, without forcing this in any way, you just begin to notice that and to allow your attention to rest with the breath. That's all there is to it.

There will be space do that practice in a moment. You might want to prepare for that now by reading Box 1.

BOX 1: POSTURES FOR MEDITATION

On my own public courses and in the work I do teaching mindfulness in organisations, we meditate sitting in chairs and nothing special is needed to do that. The main thing is to find a posture that works for you. One that is comfortable, alert and dignified – and which takes the limits of your body into account. If need be you can do all the meditation practices on this course lying down, although some people find that they tend to fall asleep when they do that.

Sitting in a Chair

If you decide you want to meditate sitting in a chair, it's best to choose one that is more or less upright. An office chair, which can be adjusted for height and seat angle, can be a good choice, as is a dining or kitchen chair.

As you see in the illustrations overleaf, it's good to have your back more or less upright. Not stiff or stretched – just gently rising up from the seat. With some chairs, especially those whose seat tilts you backwards, causing the lower spine to slump, it might help to lift the back legs off the

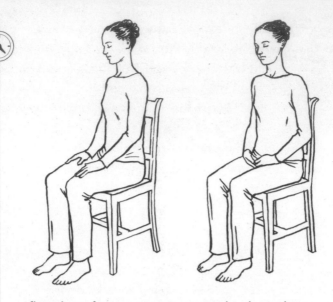

floor by a few centimetres, using books perhaps, or blocks of wood or an old towel or blanket rolled up. If your legs are a bit short for the chair, you might rest your feet on a cushion or two, or on a folded blanket.

Let your hands rest where they feel most comfortable – on your thighs perhaps, or in your lap.

There's something to be said for adopting a more or less symmetrical posture if that's comfortable for you. That can encourage an attitude of alertness and poise. See what it's like to slump in a chair with your legs crossed and then see what it's like to sit more upright, square to the floor, feet planted symmetrically on the floor in front of you – a bit like the illustration above. Does that leave you feeling more poised and alert?

When you adopt the posture you're going to use for the meditation, you send a signal from the body to the mind that this is different. 'Here I am being attentive; relaxed and alert.'

Not everyone can sit comfortably cross-legged. If you

want to sit like that, it's really important that you have your knees supported. To do that, you'll probably want to lift your bottom off the floor by sitting on one or two firm cushions.

With your knees on the floor and your bottom supported by cushions, you have three points of contact with the floor – and that's pretty stable. If your knees don't comfortably rest on the floor you can easily strain the base of your spine. If you really want to sit in this way and your knees don't readily reach the floor, even when you lift your bottom several centimetres up on a good base of cushions, you might try lightly wedging one or two cushions under each knee.

Your hands can rest on your knees, on your thighs or in your lap.

Some people who choose to sit this way wrap a blanket or shawl around their waist, roll the top of it down a few rolls, and then tuck their hands into the top of that. This can

help to support the weight of your arms and it might stop your shoulders dragging forwards and down.

You might also want to sit on a mat or folded blanket that gives some padding under your feet.

Some people like to kneel. You can do that astride a few cushions, such as in the picture on the facing page.

Kneeling or sitting on the floor

If you decide to meditate by kneeling or sitting on the floor, you can also use a meditation stool or bench, such as the one illustrated opposite (top).

Benches like this are easily available online. Try searching online for 'meditation bench' and see what turns up. Again, some people who choose to sit this way wrap a blanket or shawl around their waist, and you might also want to sit on a mat or folded blanket as described above.

If you're going to sit cross-legged or kneel on the floor, the height of the cushions or the bench you sit on can make a really important difference. If it's too low, your

lower spine slumps naturally outwards; if it's too high, your spine curves uncomfortably inwards. If you're sitting on the floor, be sure to take a few moments to get your height right. There may be quite a bit of trial and error involved here and it may even take a few weeks to find the height that works best for you. You can adjust the height of cushions by adding or subtracting a few cushions or folded blankets from a small stack and you can adjust the sitting height of a bench by placing cushions or folded blankets between your bottom and the bench.

Perfect Comfort Is not Available

Do take the time to experiment and find the posture that works best for you. You can keep on making adjustments for quite a while till you find what works best. But remember – we're all just human beings with human bodies and there's always going to be a limit. You'll never find the perfect posture that eliminates the discomforts that come from having a body in the first place. That's just how it is, so your task here is to find a posture that's more or less workable and then put your quest for comfort to one side and get on with the practice.

MINDFULNESS OF BREATHING MEDITATION

Get yourself set up to meditate somewhere where you'll be comfortable and undisturbed. Take up the posture you'd like to use to begin with and, when you feel ready, play the track entitled 'Mindfulness of Breathing (10-Minute Version)' (⬇4 ◔10 mins).

If you don't feel ready to do the actual practice right now, you can read a short description of the practice in Box 2.

BOX 2: MINDFULNESS OF BREATHING MEDITATION

Settling

Give yourself whatever time you need to settle into the posture you're going to use for this meditation. There is no rush here and a little time spent settling before you begin to meditate can make a real difference to what you find when the more formal practice begins.

Allow your eyes to close if that is comfortable for you. If you prefer, you might leave your eyes open, letting your gaze fall, unfocused, on the floor 4 or 5 feet in front of you.

Setting Your Intention

Take a moment or two to remind yourself of your intentions. This is a time just for you and you're going to use this time to meditate – not to plan or dream or think about a problem. Of course these things might come up. But set the intention now to bring your attention back to the breath whenever you notice that the mind has wandered. And set the intention too to be gentle and kind towards your wandering mind.

Bringing Awareness to the Body

Bring your awareness to the physical sensations in your body right now, maybe focusing your attention on the sensations of touch, contact and pressure where the body makes contact with the floor and with whatever you are sitting on. Spend a few moments really exploring these sensations.

Focusing on the Sensations of Breathing

When you're ready, shift your awareness to the changing patterns of sensation in the body as the breath moves in and out.

You might let your attention rest with the sensations of slight stretching at the belly with each in-breath, and on the sensations of gentle release there with each out-breath. Or you might find that the breath is more obvious to you from the movement of the ribs or from sensations in the chest or throat or nose.

Wherever you find yourself attending to the breath, see what it's like to rest your attention there for the full duration of the in-breath and the full duration of the out-breath, perhaps noticing the slight pauses between breaths.

There's no need here to try to control the breathing in any way – just let the breath breathe as it does. Even if it seems to be a bit clunky at first, there's no special way you should be breathing. It's simply a matter of gently keeping your attention with the breath – however it is.

As best you can, bring this same attitude of allowing to the rest of your experience – there's nothing to be fixed here, no particular state to be achieved. See what it's like to simply let your experience *be* your experience – without needing it to be anything other than it is.

And When the Mind Wanders . . .

Sooner or later (usually sooner), the mind will wander away from the focus on the breath to thoughts, planning and daydreams – whatever . . . This is perfectly all right. It's just what minds do: it's not a mistake or a fault.

When you notice that your attention is no longer on the breath, in that moment you're once again aware of your experience. You might briefly acknowledge where the mind has been, perhaps making a very light mental note: 'Ah yes, that was thinking . . .' and then gently escort your awareness back to the sensations of breathing.

Whenever you notice that the mind has wandered, and it will most likely happen over and over and over again, briefly acknowledge where the mind has been and then gently and kindly bring your attention back to the breath.

Even if you find yourself getting irritated with the practice or with your wandering mind, keep coming back to an attitude of kindliness to your awareness, perhaps seeing the repeated wanderings of the mind as opportunities to bring patience and a gentle curiosity to your experience.

Do This for 10 Minutes

Continue with the practice for 10 minutes or so, perhaps reminding yourself from time to time that the intention here is simply to be aware of your experience in each moment, using the breath as an anchor to gently reconnect with the here and now each time you notice that the attention has wandered.

REMEMBERING AND FORGETTING

We set out to do a practice like the mindfulness of breathing meditation with the intention of paying attention to the breath with an attitude of gentle kindliness towards whatever we experience.

There are three key terms here: intention, attention and attitude. We forget each of these and then we remember them. Then we forget. Then we remember. Over and over.

Here's how it goes.

We're given an instruction . . .

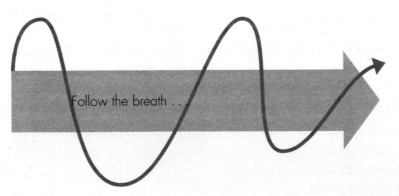

Follow the breath . . .

And because of how we've grown up, most of us will set out to 'get that right'!

It's very natural to think that there is always a right way and a wrong way of doing things. There is a right way to spell and a right way to add figures. There are all the manners and customs we learned to follow – right ways and wrong ways: thousands and thousands of them.

So when you're given an instruction in meditation, such as 'follow the breath', it's only natural to think that there is a right way of doing this. If you can keep your attention with the breath – in the case of the illustration above, within the bandwidth indicated by the shading inside the arrow – then you're 'doing it right'. And whenever your attention wanders outside that bandwidth, then you're 'getting it wrong'.

But here's what actually happens to almost everyone when they first engage with this practice.

Your attention wanders off on a journey of its own . . .

Follow the breath . . .

YOU FORGET AND REMEMBER
YOUR INTENTION

You set out to meditate – to pay attention to the breath, just for 10 minutes or so – and very soon you forget to do that. You lose that intention and instead you begin to use the opportunity of a few quiet moments to do a bit of planning. You review your to-do list, mentally rehearsing all the things you need to get done today. You're lost in that for a few moments and then somehow you remember – you intended to meditate – so you put the list aside and come back to the meditation. Soon, though, you forget that intention and instead you start a little dream: 'Hmmm . . . If I won the lottery . . . what would I spend the money on . . .?' So you dream for a bit, then you remember your intention, you come out of the dream and come back to the meditation. Then you forget your intention and begin to nod off. You settle into a half doze and go with that for a while, then you remember your intention, you straighten up, perhaps, maybe half open your eyes, and come back to the meditation.

Over and over – you forget and remember your intention to meditate.

YOU FORGET AND REMEMBER
TO PAY ATTENTION

You set out to pay attention to the breath, but very soon something else comes along and takes your attention. Maybe there's a noise from outside the room where you're practising. That grabs your attention right away and you begin to wonder what made the noise. What does it mean? Maybe it's a fire engine going by. You start to wonder where the fire is . . . Then you remember to pay attention to the breath and you bring your mind back. Then you become aware of a twinge in your lower back and you forget about the breath as your attention goes there. Maybe you start to think about that: 'Why is my back hurting right now? I wonder if it is because of the way I was carrying that heavy bag last week . . .' Then you remember the breath and draw your attention back.

Over and over – you forget and remember to attend to the breath.

YOU FORGET AND REMEMBER THE ATTITUDE

You set out with the intention of bringing your attention to the breath with an attitude of kindness and curiosity. But very soon you forget that attitude. Your mind keeps wandering and you begin to get annoyed with yourself – 'Come on, this isn't rocket science, just follow the breath. Why can't I do something as simple as that?' Then you remember the attitude and you come back to a kinder approach – 'Well yes, minds wander, that's fine, just allow it . . .' and you stay with that for a bit until maybe there's a noise outside again – perhaps a pneumatic drill starts up in the road a few blocks down. 'This city! It's so noisy! How is anyone supposed to meditate or even do anything! They're so inconsiderate, doing those road works at the weekend when we're trying to relax . . .' And then you remember the attitude – gentle, kindly, curious, allowing – so you soften around the noise, you stop trying to defend yourself against it and maybe the rhythm even becomes a soothing beat in the background. Then something starts to niggle in the intonation of the meditation instruction you're listening to. You forget the attitude and you start to get a little irritated with the instruction.

Then you remember the attitude, drop your irritation and settle back into the meditation.

Over and over – you forget and remember the attitude you're seeking to bring to the meditation.

Now here's the really great thing: each time you forget is another opportunity to remember. And each time you remember it's as if you're laying down tiny deposits in the neural pathways connected with sustained intention, sustained attention and an attitude of kindness and curiosity.

The idea that the brain is changed by our patterns of behaviour is well known these days. For example, London taxi drivers who have to memorise thousands of routes around London have significantly greater than average brain grey-matter volume in the parts of their brains that are specialised for navigation. This capacity of the brain to reshape and rewire itself in response to behaviour is called 'neuroplasticity', and the secret of neuroplasticity is repeated behaviour over time. If you do something just a few times, that might not have much impact. But if you do it thousands and thousands of times, you begin to restructure your brain.

Most people who undertake a mindfulness course and keep up the home-practice requirement over eight weeks will find their mind wandering thousands and thousands of times. That means thousands and thousands of opportunities to remember their *intention* to pay *attention* with an *attitude* of gentle and kindly curiosity.

People often say, 'Oh, I can't meditate – I tried it, but I can't empty my mind,' or 'I just can't stop my thoughts.' I hope you'll see now that this really isn't the point. The point is simply to notice and come back, notice and come back – over and over and over. Each time you forget, whether it's in the area of intention, attention or attitude, is an opportunity to come back, and each time you come back – each time you remember, it's as if you're laying down those vital deposits in the neural pathways you want to develop.

Each act of forgetting and then remembering is like moving weight in a gym. Tiny step by tiny step, over and over, you're building mental and emotional muscle.

What is more, each time you do this practice you're slowly cultivating another quality of awareness – you're cultivating mindfulness. It's not about stopping your thoughts so much as becoming *aware* of them. When you're more aware of what's moving in your mind from moment to moment, more aware of your thoughts, feelings, sensations and impulses, then you can gradually begin to exercise more choice around them.

BOX 3: FOUR KEY SKILLS

The mind wanders and you bring it back – over and over. As a result, you begin to develop, among other things, four key skills.

1. The Skill of Seeing that Your Attention Isn't Where You Want It to Be

In daily life our mind often wanders and we don't notice that it has. You may be sitting at your desk, for example, planning your week's work, but gradually your attention wanders off and you start thinking about the holiday you want to book when you get home that night. Then you begin to think about your dry-cleaning, you make a note to remember to pick up your clothes on the way home, then you start to plan what you're going to eat this evening . . . and so on.

With mindfulness training, you'll become more adept at noticing where your attention is, from moment to moment.

2. *The Skill of Unpicking Your Attention from Where You Don't Want It to Be*

You might have noticed how your thoughts, dreams and mental wanderings often come to you with a kind of stickiness – maybe even a degree of compulsion. Your mind keeps going back to your to-do list, or to thoughts about events in the past or events yet to come. You may be anxious about what's coming and regretful about the past, or you may be pleased and delighted by what's to come and OK with what's been. But, however such things show up for you, they can often be quite hard to let go of.

With mindfulness training it gradually becomes easier to see these mechanisms at work and to let go of them, unpicking your attention from the past or future.

3. *The Skill of Placing Your Attention Where You Want It to Be*

Over and over again on this course you'll find your mind has wandered. Over and over again you bring it back to your chosen focus. If you do the home practice regularly you'll gradually build the neural pathways associated with sustained attention.

4. *The Skill of Keeping Your Attention Where You Want It to Be*

Gradually over time your attentional 'muscles' start to build.

With mindfulness training you become better able to maintain some degree of sustained, present-moment attention, better able to place and maintain your attention where you want it to be. It just takes time, patience and a gentle persistence.

Be Gentle With Your Wandering Mind

Minds wander and it's easy to get irritated with yourself. But none of that helps. You just need to gently and kindly draw your attention back to where the practice guidance suggests. Just do the practices and be patient with yourself. In important ways there's actually nothing to be achieved here. All you're doing is noticing what your mind gets up to. And the moment that you notice that, even if you're hundreds of miles away from where the meditation guidance was suggesting your attention might be, then you're mindful again. Mindfulness is simply about noticing what's actually going on – in each moment.

BOX 4: MINDFUL ATTITUDES

In no particular order, here are a number of attitudinal qualities associated with mindfulness training that I hope will begin to emerge for you as you engage with this course.

NON-JUDGING. When you're mindful, you simply let what is here be what is here. You attend to each present moment without evaluation or categorisation. Non-judgement isn't the same as not being able to discern what is most appropriate. In fact, non-judgement opens the way to discernment because when you're able to let what is the case be the case, then you can decide more consciously what to do about it.

NON-STRIVING. Mindfulness practice isn't goal-oriented. You just practise, without being attached to any particular outcome. There's nothing to be achieved. You just pay attention – as far as you can.

NON-ATTACHMENT. In formal mindfulness practice, you let go of grasping and clinging to any outcome, simply allowing the process to unfold.

ACCEPTANCE. What turns up, turns up. When you're practising, you simply acknowledge things as they are in each present moment.

PATIENCE. Mindfulness practice can't be rushed. Everything unfolds in its own time.

TRUST. With practice, you begin to trust your unfolding experience. It is what it is and you're much more able *to be with it* as it is.

OPENNESS. When you're mindful, you see things afresh, as if for the first time.

CURIOSITY. With mindfulness, you begin to discover a spirit of interest, investigation and exploration. In each new moment there's something to discover.

LETTING GO. With mindfulness, you learn not to cling to passing thoughts, feelings, sensations and impulses. They come and they go.

GENTLENESS. There is a considerate and tender quality to mindfulness. But it's not passive, undisciplined or indulgent. Rather, there's an overall attitude of kindly open-heartedness.

NON-REACTIVITY. When you're mindful, you begin to respond to things with consciousness and clarity instead of automatically reacting in a habitual, conditioned way.

LOVING-KINDNESS. Gradually, a bit more friendliness, benevolence and even love can begin to spread through your experience.

UNDERSTANDING THOUGHTS
AND FEELINGS

As you will have noticed in the mindfulness of breathing meditation, the mind just keeps on chattering. We run a kind of inner
monologue and often that monologue involves a commentary on
what you're experiencing. This isn't right or wrong, it's just what
we do. But it can be helpful to see some of the mechanisms that
play themselves out in that commentary.

Here's an exercise that might begin to cast some light on how
this sometimes works.

Get comfortable, close your eyes and imagine this scenario:

- You're walking along the road one day.
- On the other side of the road you see someone you
  know.
- You smile and wave.
- The other person doesn't seem to notice and they just
  walk by.

What thoughts, feelings, sensations and impulses came up for you
as you imagined that scenario?

Just notice these for a moment before reading on.

When we do this exercise with a group in a typical mindfulness
course, here are some of the things we might hear:

Thoughts	Feelings	Sensations	Impulses
What have I done to upset her?	Worry	Tight stomach	Run after her and find out.
I know nobody likes me . . .	Loneliness	Hollowness	Keep trudging.
That's right, ignore me!	Anger	Tight jaw	Scowl back!
He's preoccupied. Is he OK?	Concern	Slight furrowing on brow	Get in touch later.

In situations like the one you just imagined, we all have different responses and it's likely that each of us will also respond differently each time, depending on the mood we bring to the situation. But notice what goes on here.

1. There is an event.
   In this case, you walk down the street, you see someone you know walking on the opposite side of the road, you smile and wave . . . and they just keep walking.

2. You interpret the event.
   'I've upset her . . .'
   'Nobody likes me . . .'
   'She's ignoring me . . .'
   'He's preoccupied . . .'

3. Your interpretation gives rise to different feelings.
   There may be feelings of worry, loneliness, anger or concern.
      These thoughts and feelings in turn affect other parts of our experience – they give rise to different body sensations and to different impulses or behaviours.

So you get a picture of experience a bit like this:

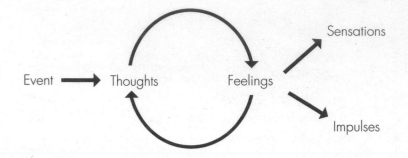

This is just how we process events. It's not right and it's not wrong – it's just how the mind works. But when all of this happens on automatic pilot, as it so often does, then you could describe it as a process of 'reaction'. An event occurs – someone walks along the road without responding to your wave – and you react: you become sad, worried, angry or whatever.

The inner monologue, the constant chatter that you notice when you sit down to meditate, colours, and is in turn coloured by, the way you experience the world. It's often quite hard to spot that. Events happen, we interpret them and we react really quickly. Imagine you're rushing to get a train on a crowded station platform and someone bumps forcefully into you. You instantly react with irritation or even anger, and then you notice their dark glasses and white stick, see that they have a visual impairment, and instantly your irritation or anger is replaced by a sense of concern for them. It can be that quick.

With eight weeks of mindfulness practice you're not going to stop reacting altogether. But as you begin to practise and to notice your inner monologue a bit more you'll find yourself reacting less often. Mindfulness training opens up choice. Instead of just re-acting you find that you begin to 'respond' a bit more. Reactions are largely unconscious, whereas responses come more from a place of awareness and conscious choice.

BOX 5: STREAM 1
HOME PRACTICE FOR WEEK TWO

- Practise the body-scan meditation again for at least six days of the coming week. Use 'The Body Scan (Longer Version)' (⬇2 ⊙35 mins) for guidance. As before, don't expect to feel anything in particular from doing the practice, rather – as best you can – put aside all expectations about it. Just let your experience be your experience.

- At a different time, practise 10 minutes of mindfulness of breathing meditation for six days. Use 'Mindfulness of Breathing (10-Minute Version)' (⬇4 ⊙10 mins) for guidance. Being with your breath in this way each day provides an opportunity to become aware of what it feels like to be connected and present in the moment without having to do anything.

- Complete the pleasant-events diary (*see page 87*). Make one entry per day. Use this as an opportunity to become more fully aware of the thoughts, feelings, sensations and impulses that come with one pleasant event each day. Notice these and record them as soon as you're comfortably able to. For example, you might try to record any actual words or images that occurred with your thoughts, or the precise nature and location of bodily sensations. But don't strain at this – it's just a guide to help you to notice.

- Choose a new routine activity to be especially mindful of – your first cup of tea or coffee; brushing your teeth; showering; drying yourself; getting dressed; your walk to the bus, train or car; eating – anything that you do every day. Again, just make a point of knowing what you are doing as you are actually doing it.

BOX 6: STREAM 2
HOME PRACTICE FOR WEEK TWO

- Practise the body-scan meditation again for at least six days of the coming week. Use 'The Body Scan (Shorter Version)' (⬇3 ⏱15 mins) for guidance. As before, don't expect to feel anything in particular from doing the practice, rather – as best you can – put aside all expectations about it. Just let your experience be your experience.
- At a different time, practise 5 minutes of mindfulness of breathing meditation for six days. Use 'Mindfulness of Breathing (5-Minute Version)' (⬇5 ⏱5 mins) for guidance. Being with your breath in this way each day provides an opportunity to become aware of what it feels like to be connected and present in the moment without having to do anything.
- Complete the pleasant-events diary (*see page 87*). Make one entry per day. Use this as an opportunity to become more fully aware of the thoughts, feelings, sensations and impulses that come with one pleasant event each day. Notice these and record them as soon as you're comfortably able to. For example, you might try to record any actual words or images that occurred with your thoughts, or the precise nature and location of bodily sensations. But don't strain at this – it's just a guide to help you to notice.

- Choose a new routine activity to be especially mindful of – your first cup of tea or coffee; brushing your teeth; showering; drying yourself; getting dressed; your walk to the bus, train or car; eating – anything that you do every day. Again, just make a point of knowing what you are doing as you are actually doing it.

BOX 7: PLEASANT-EVENTS DIARY

Notice one pleasant event each day (see table overleaf).

Day	What was the experience?	How did your body feel – in detail – during the experience?	What feelings came along with the event?
Example	On the way to work, stopping to catch the scent of a shrub.	Shoulders dropped, chest opened. Feeling of a smile.	A small feeling of joy and optimism.
Mon			
Tues			
Wed			
Thurs			
Fri			
Sat			
Sun			

What thoughts went through your mind at the time?	What impulses came along with the event?	What are you thinking right now, as you write this?
Oh at last – spring is on its way.	Just to stop for a moment and enjoy it.	Yes – spring is on its way. How good.

WEEK

THREE

MINDFULNESS OF THE BODY MOVING

COMING HOME TO YOUR BODY

On this course you pay a lot of attention to your body. That's because the body plays such an enormous part in your life. Even very slight changes to it can have a significant impact on how you feel and how you think.

In a famous study conducted in 1988, participants were told to hold a pencil between their teeth while rating the degree of humour in cartoons. One group were instructed to hold the pencil lengthways between their teeth in a way that forced their mouths to mimic a smile. The others were instructed to hold it between their lips without touching the pencil with their teeth. That forced their facial muscles to contract, resulting in a frown. The authors of the study hypothesised that participants who were led to smile would judge the cartoons as funnier than participants who were led to frown – which is exactly what happened.

What happens in your body affects what goes on in your mind and the good news is that if you change your relationship to your body you can make really beneficial changes to your life.

These days many of us spend so much time in our heads that we can forget that we have a body at all. All of our attention can become focused on thinking, planning, analysing, remembering, comparing and brooding. That excessive focus can, in time, undermine our well-being – and it's not getting any easier. As the digital world becomes ever more sophisticated, alluring and demanding of our attention, more and more of our lives are lived virtually and we can go about our lives as if we were digital clouds on sticks rather than fully embodied human beings.

On top of all this, some of us don't like our bodies very much. The media all around us present us with images of unattainable bodily perfection and we may come to think we're not thin enough, strong enough, young, tall or attractive enough.

And somewhere in the back of our minds we all know that one day our bodies will let us down dramatically – because bodies don't last forever.

The result is that often we don't treat our bodies with very much kindness. We may become slightly estranged from them, ignoring the messages they send us. That can give rise to a deep dislocation, right at the heart of our being, because, if the mind and the body are one organism, then to ignore the body is to ignore a huge part of ourselves.

Some of the emotionally charged thoughts that cause distress have their first faint stirrings in the body. On this course, you'll learn to read these more quickly and accurately, bringing a quality of gentle and friendly curiosity to what you find in the body from moment to moment. In that way you'll learn to 'come home' to your body and re-establish an old connection that modern life so easily disrupts. You'll learn to read your body more accurately and that can tell you a lot about what's going on – with yourself, others and the world around you.

MINDFUL STRETCHING

In the first two weeks of the course you meditated lying down with the body scan and you did a sitting meditation in the mindfulness of breathing meditation. Now we're going to practise mindfulness

in movement, bringing that same quality of present-moment attention to the sensations in your body when you stretch it.

There are a number of immediate health and well-being benefits
that come from stretching. Many of us spend so much of our time
sitting still, and this can have really adverse health consequences.
In fact, a study published in 2012 found that the longer you spend
sitting down every day, the higher your risk of dying prematurely,
even if you engage in regular daily exercise. So with mindful
stretching you begin a process of bringing mindfulness into movement.

WORKING THE EDGE

For many of us, these stretches will begin to take us to the edge
of our comfort zone – and that's no bad thing. This isn't because
in some kind of punitive way mindfulness teachers think that 'if it
doesn't hurt it isn't doing you good'. Quite the opposite. The idea
here is to begin a mindful – and therefore gentle and kindly –
exploration of the *edges* of that comfort zone, because it's at that
edge that really fruitful experiences can take place.

Much of the time, we arrange our lives – physically, mentally
and emotionally – so that we stay within a familiar zone of comfort. The foods we eat, the places we go, the thoughts we allow,
the people we associate with, the way we dress, the movements
we make: all of these settle in time into a pattern of comfortable
familiarity. The known, the familiar – even if it's often a painful
place to be, at least it's ours.

BOX 1: THE OLD LADY AND THE FISH BASKET

There was once an old lady who lived by the shore.

She made her living by buying fish from the fishermen there and carrying them to the town several miles from the coast where she set out her stall in the local market, selling fresh fish from her basket. She had good friends at the market, especially the flower seller who had the stall next to hers, and these two old friends would laugh and gossip together all day.

Life was good. There was only one problem – the bandits. The road between the coast and the market town was notoriously bandit infested and anyone coming home in the dark, especially an old lady who had earned several coins selling fish in the market, was easy prey for them.

For that reason, the fish seller made sure always to leave the market before dusk so she could get home to her safe hut by the shore before it grew dark. The road was safe in the daytime. There were too many people about for the bandits to operate.

One day, though, she got so absorbed in her conversation with her friend, they were having such a good time together, that she quite forgot the time and suddenly she looked up. It was growing dark.

'Oh no,' she said, 'the bandits! I don't dare walk home now. What shall I do?'

'Don't worry yourself, dear,' her friend the flower seller replied, 'there's plenty of room at my place here in town. Come home with me. You can bed down in the room where I store my flowers.'

So the two friends spent a happy evening together – chatting and laughing.

Come bedtime, the fish seller was given a bedroll and a quilt in the flower storeroom and she turned in for the night. But she couldn't sleep. She tossed and turned – there was no comfort to be found anywhere.

And then she suddenly realised – it was the sweet smell of the flowers. That's what was disturbing her. So she took her smelly old fish basket, with its comforting smell of old fish, put it over her head, and quickly drifted off to sleep.

That's how it often goes for us. We're often only comfortable with the familiar, preferring our sometimes smelly, familiar old fish baskets to the sweet scent of flowers.

Part of this week's formal mindfulness home practice is to engage in a routine of mindful stretching. As you do that, you'll begin to discover your edge. This is an opportunity to gently drop your defences and see what it's like just to experience your body as it is in each moment, noticing any tendency to compete with yourself or with imagined others.

See if you can find a way to work with this process that brings you to an edge but not over it. Always treat yourself with kindness and consideration. If a stretch feels too demanding, see how you can work with it in a way that is right for you in particular, because all of our edges are different – we're all working with the very particular circumstances of our own bodies. There can be no 'one size fits all' here – make your own decision. Be challenging, but above all be kind.

The bodily discomfort you encounter when you practise mindful stretching provides an ideal situation to learn how to approach the difficult and unwanted with curiosity, gentleness, kindness and courage. The skills you learn in this situation of physical discomfort can be applied later to situations of mental or emotional discomfort.

Imagine having your hands above your head, stretching upwards with your whole body, and it begins to feel uncomfortable in your shoulders and upper arms.

One possibility – the avoidance option – is to back off as soon as you feel any discomfort. In such circumstances you might immediately lower your arms, or take your attention to some other part of the body – maybe out of the body altogether, perhaps into a stream of thoughts or images.

Another possibility – the unkind option – is to grit your teeth, tell yourself you just have to put up with the increasing pain and discomfort and not make a fuss, as if that were actually the aim of the practice. In that way you might put even more effort into pushing yourself to stretch further. In this case, it can be common to 'numb out' from any awareness of the physical sensations in that part of the body where the discomfort is located.

Mindfully working the edge involves taking a third option and one that may feel a bit counter-intuitive at first. Instead of avoiding or pushing harder, see what it's like to adopt an 'approach' and 'allowing' attitude. Try bringing a spirit of gentle allowing to each moment, using each stretch as an opportunity to extend your ways of relating to discomfort, striking a balance between the tendency to withdraw at the first sign of discomfort, which would just reinforce any avoidant tendencies you may have, and forcing yourself to meet some standard of endurance that you have set for yourself in a driven mode of mind.

You can find that balance by a process of trial and error. As best you can, try directing your attention right into the area of intensity, using the breath as a vehicle to bring awareness into that region, just as you did in the body scan.

Then, with a gentle curiosity, explore what you find there. Notice your body sensations, fluxing and changing as they do. Sense them directly, maybe focusing on how they change in intensity over time.

The idea here isn't to hold a posture until it's painful. Rather, the intention is to move into a zone where you experience the limit of your movement in any stretch or posture and to linger there for a time, without forcing or pushing through strong sensations, keeping your attention on the sensations themselves. See what it's like to focus on the actual physical qualities of these sensations, on any sense of tightness, holding, burning, trembling or shaking, breathing with these sensations. Let your thoughts about what it means to feel these things simply come and go in awareness.

With these stretches, you can find the right zone for 'working the edge' by varying the stretch itself. This can give you some sense of control. It can give you a way to take a gentle and kindly orientation towards yourself while still learning how to do things differently.

Pain and discomfort are a part of life. To one extent or another everyone's body will produce physical pain from time to time. For some that can be severe and chronic and we all have to deal with mental and emotional pain to different degrees. None of that can be avoided. By learning to work at the edge you may come to see that when pain shows up you can take care of yourself by moving *towards* whatever you're feeling, embracing it with mindful awareness and using the same qualities of kindness and gentle investigation that you bring to exploring the intensity of a stretch.

In these stretches, don't try to force things beyond your limit. Instead, see what it's like to move towards and embrace any intensity that arises until you sense that you've reached your current tolerance limit. Then, intentionally and with care, shift your attention from the region of greatest intensity, and focus elsewhere, ready to return to the intensity when you've gathered and regrouped your resources. It can be a bit like gradually getting your big toe into the water to test the temperature and then slowly lowering your body in. You don't have to throw yourself in all at once.

MINDFUL MOVEMENT AS A FORMAL MINDFULNESS PRACTICE

The idea here is to treat these stretches somewhat differently from the way you might previously have stretched to warm up in the gym, for example, or from what you might find at some yoga or Pilates classes. What particularly distinguishes the stretches you're going to do for home practice is that you engage in them *mindfully*.

As well as cultivating an attitude of allowing, approaching rather than avoiding any challenging sensations that may emerge, there is also a clear intention here to keep your attention in the present moment, with what's actually showing up in the body from moment to moment. As ever, the mind will wander and, when it does, just briefly notice where it went – 'Oh yes, there I was thinking again . . .' or 'Oh yes . . . planning . . .' – and then gently and kindly return the attention to the stretches and to your present-moment body sensations – whatever they are.

Mindful stretches and mindful movement can also be useful when you feel yourself sliding into an unresourceful mode of mind. You can do a few stretches and regain your clarity of mind just by attending mindfully to the body's movements and the sensations that turn up as you gently stretch yourself.

STRETCHES

There are audio instructions for the mindful-movement stretches you'll be doing for home practice this week on the download site. Choose the stretches for Stream 1 (⬇6 ⏱35 mins) or Stream 2 (⬇7 ⏱15 mins) as appropriate and you might want to have a go at doing them now, as what you've read above is still fresh in your mind. Remember, it's the mindful attitude that you bring to these stretches that is really key.

If now is not a good time for you to do a full sequence of stretches, you might try just this one. As ever and above all, do take care of yourself, only going as far as is right for you and only holding the stretch for a time that feels right.

- If you'd like to, stand up with your arms by your side. You can also do this stretch sitting down.
- Begin by getting a sense of what it feels like to be standing or sitting here right now. Feel your feet making a strong contact with the floor. Feel your height rising up, your weight going down.
- Feel the breath, moving in the body.
- Your chest is open, your belly and shoulders softened.
- When you're ready, let both arms float up away from your sides until they come to shoulder height. There should be a straightish line from your left fingertips, across the shoulders, to your right fingertips.
- Stand for a moment, breathing.
- Check in. Notice any tensing, any holding, any part of the body that's tensing up and doesn't need to. Just soften and open. Keep breathing.
- Really press those fingertips away from the body – still breathing.
- Now, lift your fingers upwards as far as they'll go, pointing your fingers up towards the ceiling while you press outwards with the palms and feel the stretch across the backs of your hands, across the palms, perhaps, along the arms. Keep breathing, keep softening, keep stretching.

- See what it's like now, to just stay with that stretch for a few moments – try letting any sensations of discomfort just *be* sensations. See what it's like to move towards them, with an attitude of kindly curiosity – allowing, letting them be just as they are. Exploring, investigating.
- And, when it's right for you, let go of the stretch and check in again. What's here now?

STRETCHES

Twisting at the waist

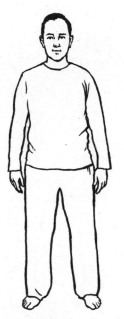

Standing and
breathing

Swinging:
twisting from the
waist, hands
slapping sides

Swinging:
twisting from the
waist, hands
slapping sides

Arms above head, thumbs locked
together, reaching up

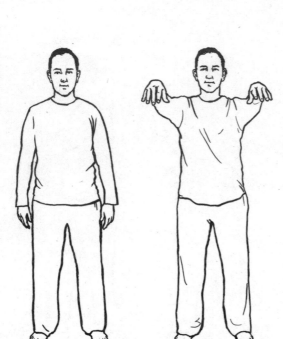

Standing and
breathing

Letting arms float up
to above your head

Locking thumbs
and reaching
upwards with
the fingers

Arms outstretched, palms pressed
out, fingers up

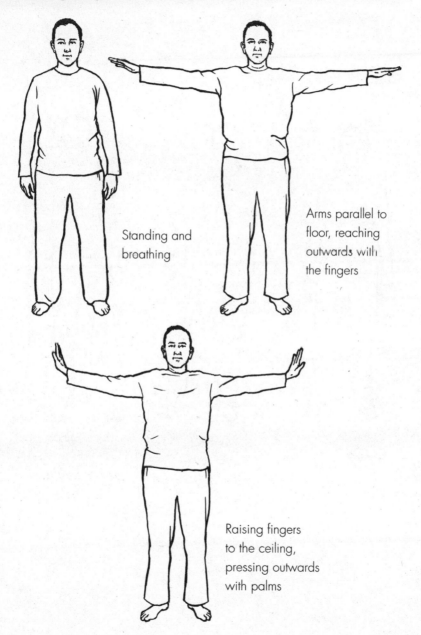

Standing and
breathing

Arms parallel to
floor, reaching
outwards with
the fingers

Raising fingers
to the ceiling,
pressing outwards
with palms

Picking fruit

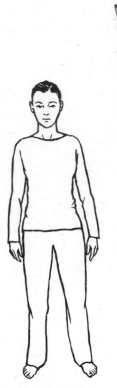

Standing and
breathing

Stretching up
with left arm
and fingers, right
heel off floor

Stretching up
with right arm
and fingers, left
heel off floor

Sideways bends

Standing and
breathing

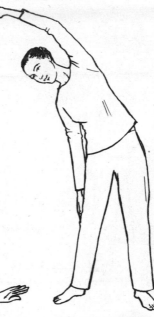

Left arm overhead,
palm facing down,
looking up towards
palm

Right arm overhead,
palm facing down,
looking up towards
palm

Shoulder rolls

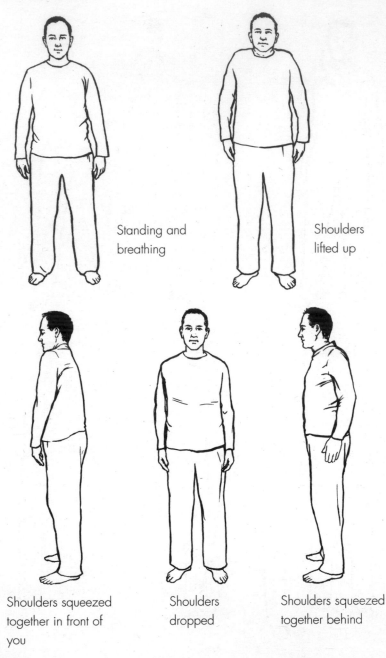

Standing and breathing

Shoulders lifted up

Shoulders squeezed together in front of you

Shoulders dropped

Shoulders squeezed together behind

Neck rolls

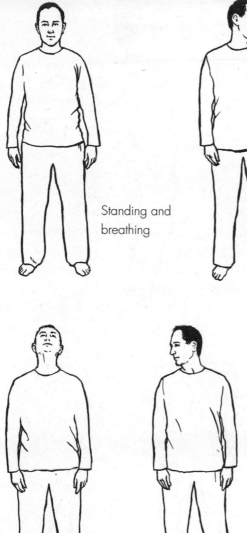

Standing and
breathing

Rolling the head
to mobilise the
neck

Circling the waist

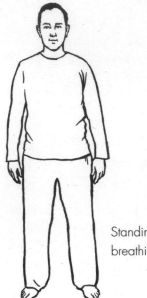

Standing and breathing

Hands in small of back, moving at the waist, opening the hips

left   behind   right

Ankle rolls

Standing and
breathing

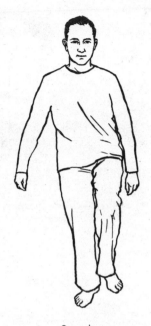

Standing on
one leg, rolling
the ankle

Forward bend

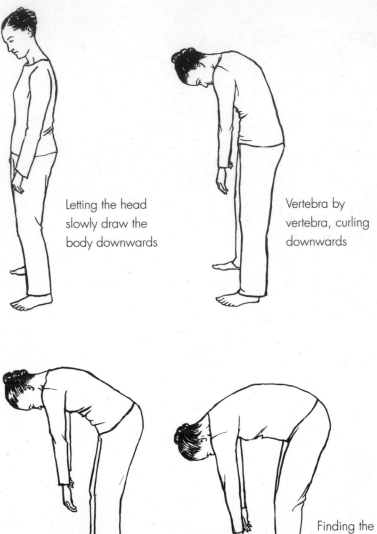

Letting the head slowly draw the body downwards

Vertebra by vertebra, curling downwards

Finding the right place for you to stop

Cat & cow stretch

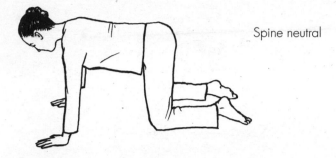

Spine neutral

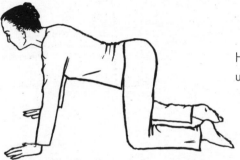

Head and bottom
up, midriff down

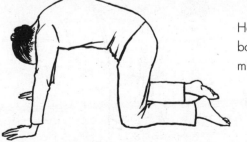

Head and
bottom down,
midriff up

Arm & leg raises

Spine neutral

Right arm forward, left foot back

Left arm forward, right foot back

Child pose

Bottom towards ankles, hands
on floor

BREATHING

Gathering air in

Standing and breathing: hands in front of navel, knees unlocked

Breathing in, pulling up . . .

Turning palms at chest height

Breathing out, floating down

Turning at the bottom

Pushing away

Standing and
breathing

Breathing in,
pulling up ...

Breathing out,
pushing away

Breathing in,
pulling back

Breathing out,
floating down

Opening wide

Standing and
breathing

Breathing in,
pulling up ...

Breathing out,
opening wide

Breathing in,
pulling back …

Breathing out,
floating down

Circling around

Standing and
breathing

Breathing in,
pulling up . . .

Following with
the eyes

Breathing
out, circling
around

BOX 2: CHANGE TAKES TIME

Some of our habitual ways of being with discomfort are deeply ingrained and it's not easy to change deep habits. Change comes over time and with practice.

Autobiography in Five Short Chapters

1. I walk down the street.
   There is a deep hole in the sidewalk.
   I fall in.
   I am lost . . . I am hopeless.
   It isn't my fault.
   It takes forever to find a way out.
2. I walk down the same street.
   There is a deep hole in the sidewalk.
   I pretend I don't see it.
   I fall in again.
   I can't believe I'm in the same place.
   But it isn't my fault.
   It still takes a long time to get out.
3. I walk down the same street.
   There is a deep hole in the sidewalk.
   I see it is there.
   I still fall in . . . it's a habit.
   My eyes are open.
   I know where I am.
   It is my fault.
   I get out immediately.
4. I walk down the same street.
   There is a deep hole in the sidewalk.
   I walk around it.
5. I walk down another street.
   Portia Nelson

The three-step breathing space is a pocket-sized meditation that you can do anywhere. It generally takes around three minutes – but that's just a rough guide and you can make it as long or as brief as you like.

The idea here is to begin to practise it three times a day for the coming week. Then, when you've got a feeling for it and know how it goes, you can begin to use it to help you deal with moments of stress. If you've had a difficult interaction with someone, for example, you can use the three-step breathing space to regain some equanimity. If you've got a challenge coming up, maybe a difficult phone call to make, you can use the three-step breathing space to help you to prepare.

BOX 3: THE THREE-STEP BREATHING SPACE

Step 1: What's Up, Right Now?
Take up an alert and dignified posture – sitting or standing. As soon as you do that you send a message from your body to your mind that you're going to make a change. 'This is different. This isn't me just sitting or standing as usual. This is me becoming more mindful.'
   Now, ask yourself:

- What's up? What's here right now?
- What are you thinking – if anything?
- What are you feeling?
- What sensations are loudest in your experience right now?
- What impulses are around?

   Just check in – thoughts, feelings, sensations, impulses. You don't need an answer to every question, it's just a rough guide to help you become more mindful of what's up for you, right now. Treat it lightly – simply acknowledging whatever emerges.

Step 2: Coming to the Breath
Having acknowledged what's up right now, gently but deliberately redirect your attention to the breath and, as far as you can, for a little while follow each in-breath and each out-breath. Just breathing, just following the breath and staying with the sensations that come with each in-breath and each out-breath.

Step 3: Moving Out Again
Now expand your awareness to include the breath and u sense of the body as a whole – breathing. Just being aware of whatever is here: the breath, the face, the body. Breathing into any tensions that may be here, opening and softening, allowing . . .

Then, when you're ready, open your eyes and gradually begin to re-engage with the world around you.

BOX 4: THE PHYSICAL BAROMETER

Some of the time we really don't know what we feel. We spend so much time in our heads that we can lose touch with other parts of our experience. My colleague Trish Bartley at the Centre for Mindfulness Research and Practice at Bangor University has developed a practice called the 'physical barometer', which is designed to help you bring a heightened awareness of feelings into your everyday life.

We don't use barometers much these days and you usually only find them in antique shops, but, if you have one or have ever seen someone consult one, you'll know that first you tap gently on the glass and then you look to see which way the needle inside the glass moves. If the needle moves up, the air pressure is rising and the weather will probably improve, and if the needle goes down, rain may be on its way. But things vary according to seasons, so predicting the weather can be quite complex.

It's the same with our bodies. We can use them to give us very sensitive information about how things are for us at any given moment.

1. Find a part of your body – maybe the chest area or the abdomen or somewhere in between the two – that for you is especially sensitive to stress and difficulty.

2. Once you have located such a place it can become your 'physical barometer'. You can tune in to it, paying attention to sensations there regularly, at different moments, every day. If you're stressed, you may notice sensations of tension or discomfort. Such sensations may be strong or faint, depending on the intensity of the difficulty. They may change as you pay attention to them. If you're experiencing ease and pleasure, tune in again: you may notice quite different sensations.

3. As you become more practised at reading your physical barometer, you may find that you start to notice subtle variations that offer you detailed and early information about how you are feeling moment by moment, long before you are aware of this in your mind.

4. Any time you tune in to your physical barometer, if you wish, you can move to doing a three-step breathing space to help you stay present with a difficult situation or with discomfort. Alternatively, you may choose just to monitor the sensations in your physical barometer moment by

moment and be with them just as they are. Just allowing things to be. Accepting, as much as you can, how things actually are and being with your changing experience, from moment to moment.

BOX 5: APPROACH AND AVOIDANCE

The prefrontal cortex, a small part of the brain just behind the forehead, plays a significant part in your overall experience of mood.

Clinical observations of people who have damage to the prefrontal cortex show that the results differ according to whether the damage is to the left or to the right side of that area. Damage to the left side can leave people unable to feel joy. They sometimes experience strong increases in sadness and uncontrollable crying. Damage to the right side, on the other hand, can leave people indifferent to injury and sometimes prone to inappropriate laughter.

Early in his career, the neuroscientist Richard Davidson (see Box 1 of the Introduction, 'A Small Digression into History', *page 10*) helped to develop the idea that the extent of activation on either the right or the left side of a person's prefrontal cortex tells you something significant about their inner experience. People with consistently higher activity in the left part of the prefrontal cortex are energised, alert, enthusiastic and joyful; they enjoy life more and have a greater sense of overall well-being. In contrast, when greater activity in the right prefrontal cortex is observed, that corresponds to people reporting experiences of worry, anxiety and sadness. At the extreme, this indicates a high risk of significant depression.

Starting in the 1970s, researchers in the field of

happiness and well-being posited the idea of a happiness 'set point' or affective style. The idea here was that by the time we become adults we experience more or less stable levels of well-being because, over time, we adapt to even the most extreme positive and negative life circumstances. If you're disposed to unhappiness, for example, and you win the lottery, you may become manic for a bit, then you may cheer up for a time, but soon you snap back and just become an unhappy rich person. On the other hand, if you're disposed to happiness and you lose an arm, you might become unhappy for a time but eventually you're likely to become a cheerful one-armed person.

Davidson's interest in meditating monks, which we discussed in the Introduction, arose from his interest in the relationship between mental training exercises, such as meditation, and the happiness set point. Could it be, he wondered, that by altering the signals that the cognitive part of the brain transmits to the emotional part, you could in a lasting way change the pattern of prefrontal activation in a way that leads to more frequent and more positive emotions?

If scientists had thus far found that people were returning to their happiness set point, was it because they were studying people who, just like almost everyone else in the West at that time, did not realise that you can build and change the brain's emotional circuitry in much the same way as you can build and change your biceps in a gym? Perhaps no one had yet tried an intervention that shifted affective style in an enduring way.

Davidson suspected that the happiness set point was movable. The question was: what moved it? This question is what took him up the Himalayas to try to study super-experienced meditators and it's what in time led a steady trickle of maroon-robed monks to pass through his laboratory at the University of Wisconsin.

The results that emerged from Davidson's studies with the monks were extreme.

When they were meditating, for example, the expert meditators showed higher levels of gamma signals than had ever been recorded in a neuroscience study before. Gamma-wave levels reflect mental effort. They appear when the brain brings together a number of elements that give rise to an 'aha!' moment of recognition – 'Oh yes . . . those white dots on the horizon I've been straining to see . . . that's an offshore wind farm, not a flotilla of yachts!' Usually these signals last for a couple of hundred milliseconds. But in the experienced meditators they lasted for up to 5 minutes. 'It was like a continuous *aha!* moment,' said Davidson. Mental training allowed the monks to produce heightened brain states associated with perception and problem-solving more or less at will while they were meditating. Even when they were not meditating they showed higher gamma activity. This hinted at what Davidson and his colleagues had been looking for in their initial expedition to the Himalayas – evidence that mental training could produce enduring brain traits. This idea was strengthened when it became apparent that the more hours of meditation training the adepts had put in the greater and more enduring the gamma signals they produced.

Other experiments, this time using fMRI, also produced unusual results, but one factor stood out from all the rest. While the monks were meditating, activity in their left prefrontal cortex swamped activity in their right prefrontal to an extent never before recorded.

As we've seen, left prefrontal activation is associated with happiness; right prefrontal activation is associated with unhappiness and states such as anxious vigilance. These results suggested that emotions could be transformed by mental training. Perhaps the happiness set point wasn't a set point after all.

It's one thing to investigate the brains of really skilled meditators but another to see if those changes can be replicated in an ordinary population group. Davidson set out to conduct such a study in collaboration with Jon Kabat-Zinn – this time studying the brains of people who had never meditated before and who were enrolled on an eight-week mindfulness course.

They delivered an eight-week mindfulness course to workers in a high-pressure biotech company in Madison, Wisconsin. One group undertook the eight-week course and a comparison group of volunteers from the company received the training later. Both groups were tested before and after training by Davidson and his colleagues. Before the course, the whole group – as with many who work in high-pressure environments – were tipped on average somewhat towards the right in the ratio for the emotional set point and complained of feeling highly stressed. The group who received the mindfulness training, however, reported afterwards that their moods had improved. They felt more engaged in their work, more energised and less anxious. This was borne out by their brain-scan results. Their left-to-right prefrontal-cortex activation ratio had shifted significantly leftwards. These results persisted at the four-month follow-up.

The subjective experience of participants accorded with that objective data. The mindfulness training, it seemed, left them feeling healthier, more positive and less stressed. Michael Slater, a molecular biologist at the company, said:

I really am an empiricist in every aspect of my life. I doubt dogma, and I test it. I do it at the laboratory bench, but also in my personal life. So this appealed to me, because I could feel the reduction in stress. I could tell I was less irritable. I had more capacity to take on more stressors. My wife felt I was easier to be around. So there were tangible impacts. For an empiricist, that was enough.

Mindfulness also improved the robustness of the meditators' immune systems. Both the mindfulness-trained group and the group who got the training later were given flu jabs. Participants in the mindfulness group produced significantly more flu antibodies in their blood after receiving the jab. The greater the leftward shift in the emotional set point, the larger the increase in the immune measure.

Eight weeks of mindfulness training produced a more robust immune system in participants. It also significantly increased their left prefrontal-cortex activation and made them happier and less stressed.

Another way of understanding part of what happened here is that the mindfulness group became more 'approach-oriented' while the group who received the training later remained somewhat 'avoidance-oriented'.

The history of these modes of mind goes back in evolutionary terms to the emergence of two distinct neurological processes: approach systems and avoidance systems. Since the 1970s, some researchers have proposed that two general motivational systems play a large part in shaping our experience: a behavioural inhibition system (BIS) and a behavioural activation system (BAS). For simplicity's sake we might call these the *avoidance system* (for BIS) and the *approach system* (for BAS).

The approach system turns us towards potential rewards. Our sense of being attracted to a person or to a piece of chocolate, as well as our desire to approach the person or chocolate, comes from this system. The avoidance system, on the other hand, sensitises us to potential punishment or danger and motivates us to avoid it. That we're fearful of rejection by someone we love, or we're afraid of snakes, along with our wish to avoid such things, comes from the avoidance system.

Davidson's earlier research showed that the approach system correlates to left prefrontal-cortex activation. It is reward-seeking and is associated with positive emotions such as hope and joy and with the anticipation of good events. The avoidance system, on the other hand, which correlates to right prefrontal-cortex activation, inhibits our movement towards goals and is associated with feelings of fear, disgust, aversion and anxiety.

There's a real evolutionary value to these systems. They play a key part in the way in which we approach things we think will be good for us and avoid things that threaten us. But genetic and life experiences can skew these mechanisms so that, as an adult human being, you may find, at one extreme, some of us have developed a chronically overactive avoidance system – leading us to be overanxious or prone to depression.

Mindfulness training, as Davidson and others have shown, can change that. It can help you become more approach-oriented. Gently, steadily, step-by-step, this course offers opportunities to move towards what is difficult and to find new ways of being with it – approaching, rather than avoiding, what you have previously found to be uncomfortable. Working the edge.

BOX 6: EMPATHY AND BODY AWARENESS

When you're better able to read what is happening in your own body, you'll also be better at reading what is going on with others. Heightened awareness of your own body and its states can increase your own levels of empathy.

For almost all of the 2.6 million years of human history up until the beginning of settled agriculture about 10,000 years ago, our forebears lived in tribal bands – usually no bigger than 150 members. They had to compete with others for scarce resources, avoid predators and spend almost all their waking hours searching for food. In that kind of harsh environment, those who were better able to cooperate generally lived longer and left more offspring. Bands that were better at teamwork generally beat those whose teamwork was weaker. Since they were more likely to survive, it is their genes we have mainly inherited, and that gives us an in-built capacity to read what is happening – 'read' one another, as we must do if we are to work skilfully together.

Humans have the capacity to read the inner states of other humans to an extraordinary extent. These capabilities are driven by three different neural systems: we have the capacity to sense – and to simulate within our own experience – other people's *actions*, their *emotions* and their *thoughts*.

The networks in your brain that are activated when you perform an action are also activated when you see someone else perform it. That gives you, in your own body, a felt sense of what others experience in their bodies. The way these networks 'mirror' the behaviour of others gives them their name: mirror neurons. Think about what happens when you see someone choking up in distress, for example. Most likely you will notice in your own body some reflection of what they are actually feeling in theirs – although usually to a lesser extent. Or think about what happens when you see a friend or family member bursting with happiness. Most likely you'll experience some of the physical components of elation for yourself.

There are emotion-related circuits forming our experience. The neural circuits that are usually active when you experience strong emotions, such as fear or anger, are sympathetically activated in you when you see others having the same feelings. That allows you to make sense of the feelings of others, so the more aware you are of your own feelings and body sensations, the better you will be at reading these in others.

Yet another set of circuits comes into play when you come to 'read' the thoughts and beliefs of other people. The prefrontal circuits involved in helping us to guess the thoughts of others work in conjunction with the circuits involved in sensing the feelings and actions of others. Together, these produce your overall perception of their inner experience.

The capacity for two people to 'feel felt' by each other is a key factor in allowing those in relationship to one another to feel vibrant, alive, understood and at peace. A significant element in your capacity to read others is your capacity to read what is happening inside yourself. The more able you are to read what is happening in your own body the more accurately you'll be able to read others.

BOX 7: NARRATIVE MODE, EXPERIENCE MODE

Norman Farb studies psychology and neuroscience at the University of Toronto, where his research focuses on the relationship between present-moment awareness and well-being.

Drawing on a variety of research findings, he notes that present-moment awareness enables people to change unconstructive or disruptive behaviour into something more constructive. But modern life is filled with distractions that fracture our attention and take us away from present-moment awareness – smartphones, the Internet, ads, social media – it's an endless list. Now, of course it's important to think beyond your immediate situation so you can plan for future events, but the habit of living in the future or the past comes at the expense of responding constructively to challenges in the present and can lead to all kinds of unwanted consequences, such as stress, anxiety and depression.

Farb used mindfulness-training techniques to look at how the practice of attending to momentary sensations can alter your sense of self and your well-being.

As we've seen, a central mechanism of mindfulness training is to use moment-by-moment body sensations as an anchor to focus your attention on the present. By investigating changes in behaviour and changes in the brain-activation network that showed up alongside a mindfulness-training programme somewhat like the one we are doing, Farb began to develop a neuroscientific model of how we come to know ourselves and the world through our physical bodies.

As you become more aware of your changing body sensations, he says, you also become better able to respond to the problems that are created or perpetuated through negative thinking. For example, we've seen how ruminating over a situation or your life circumstances can reinforce depressed mood. And we've seen how catastrophising at times of stress further reinforces the experience of anxiety. At times of challenge, on the other hand, the capacity to turn *towards* the present moment by focusing on body sensations here and now can be a powerful technique for disengaging from unresourceful ways of thinking.

In 2007 Farb and his colleagues published a study that sheds new light on our understanding of mindfulness from a neuroscience perspective. They discovered that people have two distinct ways of interacting with the world, using two different sets of networks in the brain. One network for experiencing is known as the 'default network'. It's called 'default' because it's where we default to when there's not much else going on – a bit like a car's engine running in neutral.

Imagine you're standing, waiting for a bus on a lovely sunny day. You've got nothing in particular to do, there are no immediate calls on your attention. Instead of just standing there, enjoying the feeling of sunshine on your skin, the breeze ruffling your hair and the lovely blue of the sky, you find yourself beginning to work out a menu for tonight's dinner and you become slightly anxious about your capacity to make it tasty enough for the family. That's your default network spinning. Planning, daydreaming and ruminating: we spend so much of our time lost in its constant chatter.

The default network kicks in when you think about

yourself or other people. It pulls together your 'narrative' – the story of your history and your future, and of all the people you know.

When you experience the world using this network, information from the outside world is processed through a filter of what everything means – with added interpretations.

So, standing waiting for a bus, maybe you see a young child with her mother. That makes you wonder about your own children and whether you were a good enough parent and are they OK right now? One moment you're waiting for a bus on a sunny day, the next moment you're inwardly, maybe anxiously or critically, rehearsing key moments in your life.

There's nothing wrong with the default network in and of itself, but if you only experience the world through its lens, that can have unhelpful consequences.

Farb showed that there is another way of experiencing. This is by way of simple, direct experience. The network that processes direct experience includes the insula, a brain region involved in perceiving bodily sensations, as well as those networks that are central to switching your attention. When this collection of networks is activated, you're not thinking about the past, the future, other people or yourself. In fact, you're not doing very much thinking at all. Rather, you simply experience information coming into your senses in real time.

Waiting for the bus on a sunny day, your attention is on the feeling of warmth on your skin, the breeze in your hair and your feet on the ground. You're contentedly standing there, experiencing what you experience.

These two ways of processing experience, the default-network 'narrative mode' on the one hand and the direct-experience 'experiential mode' on the other, are inversely related. In other words, the more you do one, the less you do the other. You sense (see, hear, feel . . .) much less when you're lost in thought. And when you focus your attention on simple sense experience in the moment, that reduces activation in the narrative circuitry.

So when you find your own narrative circuits spinning anxiously and you're worrying about a future stressful event or ruminating self-critically, it can be really useful to take a deep breath and focus your attention on simple experiences in the present moment – the feeling of your feet on the floor, perhaps, or even the churning sensations in your stomach. That can dramatically change the degree of activation of the narrative circuits.

The narrative circuits are really helpful for planning, setting goals and creating strategies. They enable us to create art and they enrich life enormously. But they can imprison and entrap you in unresourceful mental habits as well. When you develop your capacity to experience the world more directly, your senses come more alive and you can open the door to other ways of experiencing.

The experiential network allows you to get closer to the simple here-and-now reality of things. You begin to perceive more accurately what is actually going on around you. Taking in more real-time information, you become more flexible in how you respond to the world, less imprisoned by the past – by habits, expectations and assumptions – and more able to respond to events as they unfold.

Farb's study showed that people who practised mindfulness have a stronger differentiation between their brain's narrative and experiential pathways. They knew which pathway they were on at any time, and could switch between them more easily, whereas those who hadn't learned the skill of mindfulness were more likely to automatically engage their narrative, default networks.

BOX 8: STREAM 1
HOME PRACTICE FOR WEEK THREE

- Practise the movements on the track 'Mindful Movement (Longer Version)' (◐6 ◔35 mins) daily for six days. The point of these movements is to connect directly with the body. Working with your body in this way can allow you to experience more of yourself and to connect up your experiences of body sensations, feelings, thoughts and impulses. If you have any back or other health difficulties that may cause problems, make your own decision as to which (if any) of these exercises to do, taking good care of your body.
- At a different time practise 10 minutes of mindfulness of breathing each day. Use the track 'Mindfulness of Breathing (10-Minute Version)' (◐4 ◔10 mins) for guidance here.
- Practise using the three-step breathing space three times a day at times that you have decided in advance. For one of those times, use the track 'Three-Step Breathing Space' (◐8 ◔3 mins) for guidance. After that, try doing it on your own without guidance.
- Complete the unpleasant-events diary (*see page 139*), making one entry per day. Use this as an opportunity to become more fully aware of the thoughts, feelings, sensations and impulses that come with one unpleasant event each day. Notice these and record them as soon as you're comfortably able to. For example, you might try to record any actual words or images that occurred with your

thoughts, or the precise nature and location of bodily sensations. But don't strain at this – it's just a guide to help you to notice.

- What are the unpleasant events that 'pull you off centre' or 'get you down' (no matter how big or small)?
- What do you most not want to look at?
- Notice when you move into automatic pilot – under what circumstances does this occur?
- As best you can, try to 'capture' the moments of your day.

BOX 9: STREAM 2
HOME PRACTICE FOR WEEK THREE

- Practise the movements on the track 'Mindful Movement (Shorter Version)' (⊙7 ⊙15 mins) daily for six days. The point of these movements is to connect directly with the body. Working with your body in this way can allow you to experience more of yourself and to connect up your experiences of body sensations, feelings, thoughts and impulses. If you have any back or other health difficulties that may cause problems, make your own decision as to which (if any) of these exercises to do, taking good care of your body.
- At a different time practise 5 minutes of mindfulness of breathing each day. Use the track 'Mindfulness of Breathing (5-Minute Version)' (⊙5 ⊙5 mins) for guidance here.
- Practise using the three-step breathing space three times a day at times that you have decided in advance. For one of those times, use the track 'Three-Step Breathing Space' (⊙8 ⊙3 mins) for guidance. After that, try doing it on your own without guidance.

- Complete the unpleasant-events diary (*see below*), making one entry per day. Use this as an opportunity to become more fully aware of the thoughts, feelings, sensations and impulses that come with one unpleasant event each day. Notice these and record them as soon as you're comfortably able to. For example, you might try to record any actual words or images that occurred with your thoughts, or the precise nature and location of bodily sensations. But don't strain at this – it's just a guide to help you to notice.
    - What are the unpleasant events that 'pull you off centre' or 'get you down' (no matter how big or small)?
    - What do you most not want to look at?
    - Notice when you move into automatic pilot – under what circumstances does this occur?
- As best you can, try to 'capture' the moments of your day.

BOX 10: UNPLEASANT-EVENTS DIARY

Notice one unpleasant event each day (see table overleaf).

Day	What was the experience?	How did your body feel – in detail – during the experience?	What feelings came along with the event?
Example	On an overcrowded train, stuck on the tracks, late for work.	Tight jaw, churning stomach, tight shoulders.	Frustration, anger, restlessness.
Mon			
Tues			
Wed			
Thurs			
Fri			
Sat			
Sun			

What thoughts went through your mind at the time?	What impulses came along with the event?	What are you thinking right now, as you write this?
I'm going to have such a hassle explaining this at work – again!	Phone the CEO of the train company and scream at him!	That was quite a reaction!

WEEK

FOUR

MANAGING
REACTIONS

Some of the time you just can't help it:

- A bullying driver cuts in front of you in traffic when you're agitated and running late. You hoot, glare and begin to churn inwardly, tightly gripping the wheel and angrily muttering to yourself.
- The kids at home make one more unruly demand and you snap at them in a way that only makes things worse.
- You pass by a cake shop, slip in and buy a pastry before you've even remembered your resolution to avoid high-carb foods.
- A colleague is aggressive at work and you collapse inside yourself, losing all your potency.

What unites all of these reactions is just that – they are reactions. They emerge at lightning speed from the more primitive parts of your brain before you've been able to think things through just a tiny bit and come out with more skilful and appropriate responses.

Reactions like these are much more likely to emerge at times of stress. When you're stressed, the more primitive parts of your brain are on hyper-alert, ready to shoot first and ask questions later, and very often these hair-trigger reactions really don't serve your own or anyone else's best interests.

In each of the cases outlined above it wouldn't be difficult to imagine a smarter, more skilful response. But imagining a smarter response when you're feeling calm and reflective is one thing – coming up with one in the heat of the moment is quite another.

How do you do that?

Part of the answer lies in learning the deeply counter-intuitive skill of allowing what is difficult and uncomfortable simply to *be* difficult and uncomfortable.

When unpleasant feelings or experiences arise, the whole intuitive thrust of the mind is to get rid of them. Faced with difficulty or discomfort when on automatic pilot, we naturally react with aversion. The mindfulness approach turns this around. Instead of trying to get rid of unpleasant feelings, when you are mindful you can begin to hold such experiences in awareness. That lets you see them for what they are and it allows you to meet them with a conscious response rather than with an automatic reaction.

BOX 1: THE TWO ARROWS

In ancient times, arrows were used in hunting and also as weapons of war. If you were struck by one of them, you really felt it. Taking that as an analogy, the very early practitioners of mindfulness spoke of two arrows – the first one is physical and the second one is mental.

When the unmindful person is struck by an arrow, he or she is then very rapidly struck by a second arrow.

Imagine you're on a battlefield and you're hit by an arrow. That hurts! But then very rapidly another arrow comes flying in as your mind gets going. 'Why does this sort of thing only happen to me?' 'What's going to happen now?' 'How am I ever going to recover?' 'I knew I should never have come onto this battlefield.' 'I should have done better training!' On and on – your mind rapidly produces further arrows that add to the pain of the first one.

When the mindful person is struck by an arrow, they said in ancient times, they feel the pain of the arrow – and it stops there.

The first arrow represents the suffering that comes to all of us just from being human. Often, we don't get what we want and instead get what we don't want. And even when we *do* get what we want, it's impossible to hold on to it forever. That's part of what it means to be human. But the way in which we usually deal with the pain and difficulty that comes our way causes us to be struck by second, third, fourth and fifth arrows – and all of these are self-generated.

With mindfulness training you learn to stop doing that quite so much. By holding what is painful and uncomfortable in the space of mindful attention, the reactive process of adding further levels of pain to existing pain comes to a stop.

We tend to react to painful feelings with aversion. That's how we're wired up. We don't like pain or discomfort and we spend much of our time trying to get rid of it. To do that, we adopt a variety of strategies, many of them unconscious. We may tune out and go blank, or we get into fantasies and daydreams, or we might go on the attack, giving rise to feelings of anger, or blame. Or we may immediately look about for a fix – 'Something must be able to take this discomfort away – now!' Or else we may grasp for a new, more pleasant experience to take our unease away.

All of these reactions are ultimately unhelpful. Grasping, blanking, getting angry and so on all produce their own kinds of pain and so a vicious cycle comes into being, where unpleasant and unwanted feelings produce reactions that are themselves unpleasant – and so on.

Imagine this: you've been working till late at night and you come home feeling tired to discover that your partner has already gone to bed. So, being a kind and thoughtful person you don't turn on the lights and instead you get undressed in the dark and make your way to your side of the bed. On your way there, you stub your toe, quite painfully, on the heavy briefcase your partner left lying between the chair where you get undressed and your side of the bed.

Ouch! You experience a 'first-level' stressor – the simple physical pain of stubbing your toe. But then a 'second-level' stressor kicks in as you move on to tell yourself a story about what happened.

Maybe your story is against your partner: 'He/she is so selfish, so inconsiderate. He/she never thinks of me! There I was being so kind and considerate, but him/her? Never! I've talked about that briefcase before – what's it doing in the bedroom anyway . . .!?'

So you get into bed, angrily tug the covers over to your side of the bed, and spend much of the rest of the night tossing, turning and fuming.

Or maybe the story you tell is against yourself – how foolish not to have worn shoes, or not to have turned on the light. Or maybe it's a bit of both – you mentally attack yourself *and* your partner. In any event, your body tightens, your brow furrows, and long after the pain has faded you're still engaged with the second-level stressors.

The mindful approach, by contrast, might go like this: you stub your toe and it hurts. You sit down on the chair, give your toe a gentle rub, hold it for a few moments, wait for the pain to subside, make a mental note to raise 'briefcase in bedroom' issues with partner somewhat more forcefully in the morning, get into your side of the bed and have a good night's sleep.

Second-level stressors of one kind or another can come to affect the whole of our lives, leading to maladaptive coping strategies, such as denial, fantasy, workaholism, worry, unhelpful rumination, busyness, substance abuse, overeating and so on. Since these are all variously ineffective, they end up adding to our stress-reactions rather than diminishing them.

STRESS-REACTIONS VERSUS STRESS-RESPONSES

One of the core skills with mindfulness is learning to replace unconscious stress-reactions with conscious stress-responses.

Stressors are unavoidable, but if you respond to them with awareness it is possible to institute adaptive, healthy coping strategies as opposed to maladaptive ones. Moment-by-moment awareness lets you make more creative choices. That allows you to positively influence the flow of events rather than simply reacting automatically and so perpetuating the stress-reaction cycle.

Stress-reactions, of their nature, happen automatically and largely unconsciously. By introducing the factor of awareness into previously unconscious processes you inevitably change things. This is *the* deciding factor in whether you go down the path of stress-reaction or that of stress-response. Being mindful in the moment of stress, you are more able to recognise both the stressfulness of the situation and your impulse to react. You can learn to recognise such agitations for what they are. They are not the whole of reality, they are just bundles of passing thoughts, feelings, sensations and impulses – and that changes everything.

LEARNING TO RESPOND RATHER THAN REACT

In general, we react to unwanted experience in one of three ways:

- with indifference – switching out of the present moment and going off somewhere else in our minds
- with craving – wishing we were having experiences that we are not having right now, or trying to hold on to any pleasant experiences that we are having right now
- with aversion – wanting to get rid of unpleasant experiences that we are having right now, or trying to avoid experiences that may be coming along that we do not want

Each of these ways of reacting can cause problems, particularly the tendency to react to unpleasant feelings with aversion. The main issue is to become more aware of your experience so that you can respond mindfully rather than react automatically.

Meditation can be a kind of laboratory where, under the particular conditions you have set up, you can become aware of how you tend to react to things and also to begin to see how, instead of reacting, you might begin to do things differently.

Regularly practised, meditation gives you many opportunities to notice when you have drifted away from awareness of the moment and, with a friendly awareness, to note whatever it was that took your attention away, then gently and firmly bring your attention back to the object of that meditation, such as the breath. In this way, over and over you practise the process of losing and regaining your moment-by-moment awareness.

You can also begin to use the three-step breathing space to help you to deal with reactions. Whenever you notice unpleasant feelings, or a sense of tightening or 'holding' in the body, practising a three-step breathing space can help you to respond rather than react.

As we have seen, in order to respond rather than react, above all we need awareness. Our bodies, with all their present-moment feelings and sensations, are an invaluable anchor for our awareness. The body with all its various sensations is always there to return to when your thoughts and feelings become agitated, and a lived sense of what is going on in the body, in real time, can help you to stay focused in the present moment.

For that reason, part of the emphasis of this week's practice continues to be awareness of the body in movement.

WALKING MEDITATION

As part of this week's home practice, you'll have the chance to experiment with a walking-meditation practice. There are four traditional meditation postures: sitting, lying, standing and walking. So far we've done sitting meditation with the mindfulness of breathing, lying-down meditation with the body scan, standing meditation formed part of the mindful movement last week (just standing for a few moments, mindful of the breath and sensations in the body) and this week we complete the quartet with walking meditation.

For most of us, walking forms a huge part of our daily lives. Even if it's just a walk from a train station to your workplace, or a walk from one room to another in your home or place of work, walking is something we do pretty much unconsciously and fairly often. When you've practised a bit of walking meditation, however, some of those short opportunities for walking can turn into great moments for mindfulness practice.

BOX 2: INSTRUCTIONS FOR WALKING MEDITATION

When you're ready to practise walking meditation, find a place where you can walk for 5 to 10 paces in a fairly straight line. You'll probably want to choose somewhere where you'll not be disturbed by other people or concerned about them looking at you as you practise. It could be inside or outside.

1. Stand with your feet parallel to each other and slightly apart with your knees 'unlocked' so that they can flex slightly. Let your arms hang by your sides. You don't do this meditation with the eyes closed but you don't want to be looking around too much either, so let your gaze rest on the floor 5 or 10 feet in front of you. If it's comfortable doing so, you can let your gaze be unfocused.

2. Move your attention to whatever sensations you find where your feet meet the floor. Feel your weight going down, your height reaching up. It may be helpful to flex your knees slightly a few times to give you a clearer sense of the sensations in the feet and legs.

3. When you feel ready to begin walking, let your left heel slowly rise up from the floor. Keep your attention with sensations in your legs: noticing the sensations in the calf muscles and in the thighs and knees. Continue the movement, letting the whole of the left foot gently lift up, as your weight shifts quite naturally to the right leg. Feel the sense of weight shifting. Stay aware of sensations in the left foot and leg as you carefully swing them forwards and let the left heel come into contact with the floor. Let the rest of the left foot make contact with the floor, feeling the

weight of the body shifting forwards onto the left leg and foot, as the right heel naturally comes off the floor.

4. When your weight has fully transferred to the left leg, let the rest of the right foot lift up and swing it slowly forwards, staying aware of the changing patterns of sensations in the feet and legs as you do this. Feel your right heel making contact with the floor. Sense your weight shifting forwards onto the whole of the right foot as it is placed gently on the floor, and feel the left heel rising up again.

5. In this way, keep walking slowly through the space you've chosen, staying particularly aware of sensations in the soles of the feet and heels as they make contact with the floor as well as sensations in the legs as they swing forwards.

6. When you have gone as far as you want to in one direction, let your body make a turn – however it wants to – turning slowly around, staying aware of the complex pattern of movements involved here. Continue walking in the opposite direction.

7. Walk up and down in this way, as much as possible staying aware of sensations in the feet and legs. Feel the contact of the feet with the ground. Keep your gaze gently on the floor in front of you.

8. When you notice that the mind has wandered, and you're no longer attending to the sensations of walking, gently bring the focus of attention back to the sensations in the feet, using the sensation of contact with the floor to anchor your experience and to reconnect with the present moment. If your mind becomes agitated, it may be helpful to stop for a moment: just stand, feet together, breathing . . . giving the mind and body a chance to re-stabilise themselves, and then continue to walk.

9. Walk for 10 to 15 minutes – or longer if you wish.

10. At first, try walking at a pace that is slower than usual, giving yourself a chance to be fully aware of the sensations of walking. When you're comfortable walking slowly with awareness, you can experiment with walking faster – even quite quickly. If you feel particularly agitated, it might be helpful to begin walking quickly, with awareness, and to slow down naturally as your mind settles.

11. When chance allows, see what it's like to bring this same quality of mindfulness to your normal, everyday experiences of walking.

People often report that when they first start out with walking meditation the process is quite 'clunky' and feels forced. That's perfectly natural. When you begin to do consciously what you've always done unconsciously, it's very different and this can feel almost as if you're learning to walk again. If this happens for you, do persist. After a little while a sense of ease will most likely enter the picture as you begin to become more familiar with the processes of walking meditation.

BOX 3: WHAT IS STRESS?

A stressor is anything that causes you stress. Often we think of stressors as external demands made on us by circumstances – such as events at work or in the family – but there are also biological stressors, such as a flu virus; chemical stressors, such as too much caffeine; and internal stressors, such as the way your body reacts to the purely imagined and baseless thought of danger to someone you love.

Stressors activate you and get you going. They trigger neural networks that evolved from very primitive times to help us deal with threat or challenge, and often they serve us well.

The trouble is that sometimes they don't serve us well at all.

The Pressure–Performance Curve

It is true of all life forms that, as the demands made on an organism increase, so that organism's capacity to respond to that demand also increases – but only ever up to a certain point. Beyond a certain point, if the demands just keep building the organism's capacity to respond is overwhelmed and the organism's capacity to perform falls off – often very rapidly.

Take peas, for example. Pea shoots are killed by frosts, so some gardeners who live in cooler climates start growing their pea plants indoors while there is still the chance of an outdoor frost. If you were to do this, perhaps growing a tray of pea seedlings on a sunny windowsill indoors, and you were to brush your hand gently over the tops of the seedlings every day, they would grow stronger.

This isn't because in some mystical way peas love contact with humans and thrive as a result of that love and attention. Rather, it's because you will have agitated the plants every day and in response to that challenge they develop greater strength – growing deeper roots and more robust stems.

But if you were to get too vigorous with your brushing, or if you were to take your hand and smack down on the same tray of seedlings, you would simply kill them all.

Some level of challenge, a certain degree of stress, is

good for the plants. But too much stress, or the application of it in the wrong kind of way, is disastrous.

It's the same for human beings – as shown in the pressure–performance diagram.

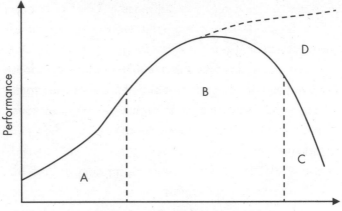

The diagram shows what happens to us as the intensity and the number of stressors we encounter increase. That's the 'pressure' we're under and, like peas, on the earlier part of the curve we respond well to it. Going to the gym, for example, or taking a vigorous walk, challenges your system and can be a healthy form of pressure. Not getting enough challenge isn't good for you. Neither is getting too much.

Zone A on the diagram is the part of the curve where you don't experience enough healthy challenge. To the extent that you are habitually inactive you are in Zone A, and that's bad for your health. Similarly, if your work doesn't involve enough challenge and stimulation and it leaves you just feeling bored all the time, you are in Zone A at work. This zone is not a very healthy place to be.

In **Zone B** you're thriving. Here there's a great balance between the demands made on you and your capacity to respond to those demands. A good trainer at the gym will push you into this zone, working you all the time nicely at the edge of your resources and so gradually building your capacity. This is also a good place to be at work or with your family or friends. Here, the work and its demands are challenging but not exhausting. You enjoy the stimulus of your work but it's not totally exhausting and it doesn't leave you constantly frazzled. In this place, your family and friends provide enough stimulus to keep relationships alive and interesting, you've not settled into dull, predictable, lifeless ways of relating.

Then there's **Zone C**. Here, you're just stressed. The demands of the task have exceeded your capacity to respond. This is like trying to run a half-marathon when you've never run more than two miles before. Or it's when the pressure at work is felt to be simply relentless and you stop being able to relax in the evening or to put the work aside when you get home. Or it's where one or more of your family or social relationships are characterised by unfulfillable demands. If you spend too long in Zone C your sleep can be badly affected and people who find themselves in this zone for too long experience all kinds of adverse health consequences: muscular-skeletal and digestive disorders, insomnia, anxiety and depression – as well as a range of diseases like hypertension, heart disease, some cancers, diabetes and much else. Persistently high levels of stress significantly increase your vulnerability to these.

The great offer of mindfulness training in this respect is that it might enable you to notice more readily when you're slipping into Zone C, into a stressed state, and it offers some practical methods for helping you to come back to equilibrium – the three-step breathing space, for example, and regular meditation practice. Practices such as these help you to calm, and create space for reflection where you can begin to choose wiser courses of action.

That brings us to **Zone D**. Zone D is the Zone of Delusion. Here, you think you're doing well, you tell yourself and others that everything's fine and you're thriving – but you're not. In Zone D you've just stopped noticing. You're persistently focused on your tasks in the short term and you've stopped noticing what's happening in yourself, to others and in the world around you.

Too much time spent in Zone D can lead to really unhappy consequences. Once you stop doing the things that actively help you to maintain or regain your equilibrium, you can enter what the psychologist Professor Marie Asberg has called an exhaustion funnel.

Think of all the things that bring some joy and some happiness into your life: the time you spend with your friends and family, time spent listening to music, going to

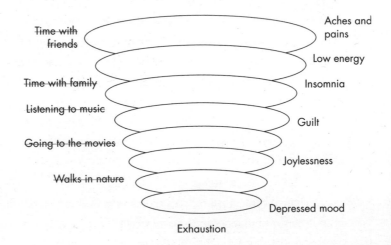

the movies or the theatre from time to time, walks in nature and so on. Everyone will have their own list of these activities.

When you're in Zones C and D, it seems that there simply isn't time for these activities and you progressively give them up. One after the other you drop the things on the left-hand side of the funnel diagram. But what you've not noticed is the extent to which they've been supporting your life and enabling you to stay on a healthy equilibrium. They seem optional but they're not. They're vital, and if you let go of too many of these things you enter the exhaustion funnel, spiralling progressively downwards towards burnout and exhaustion. When you stop doing the things that nourish you, you're left with only work and other stressors that continue to deplete your resources.

The key here is to notice the slide. When things pile up and seem to get too much, you naturally become stressed. When you notice that, you can take some action. First of all, do something like the three-step breathing space. Then you might go for a short walk, call a friend and talk things through, give yourself time for a hot bath, arrange to do one of the things on the left-hand side of the exhaustion funnel. It's noticing the signs of stress that can really help you avoid going into Zone D. When you recognise stress as stress, you can do something about it.

BROADENING THE FOCUS IN MEDITATION

We've seen this week how much value there can be in holding your experience within the space of mindful awareness. It can help you to respond and not react. The meditations you've practised so far on the course have taken a somewhat narrow focus as their object: the breath in the mindfulness of breathing, particular body sensations in the body scan. Now we're going to experiment with broadening that focus.

The sitting meditation this week will be longer than in the previous weeks. Starting with a session of mindfulness of breathing, Streams 1 and 2 will continue to sit and add in another practice – mindfulness of the breath and the body, making for a single 20-minute session of sitting meditation. After that, Stream 1 will extend still further, adding in two further elements to the practice, making for a combined 40-minute session of sitting meditation. But more about that later. For now, we'll focus on the second practice you'll be adding in – mindfulness of the breath and body.

In this practice, you begin to extend the scope of your attention from focusing on the breath to becoming aware as well of the body as a whole as you sit there breathing.

BOX 4: MINDFULNESS OF THE BREATH AND BODY

As best you can, keep your attention with the breath, as it moves in and as it moves out of the body. Perhaps feeling a sensation of slight stretching in the abdomen as the breath comes in, a sense of gentle release as it goes out. Just staying with the breath, however it shows up for you.

1. Then, allow your field of attention to expand around the breath, and begin to include in that field some of the many and various sensations throughout your body, whatever they are. Staying with the sense of breath moving in the body, allow the primary focus now to be a sense of the body as a whole – breathing.

2. You may be aware of sensations down at the feet – a sense of touch or pressure or contact. You may be aware of sensations where the body meets the seat. See what it's like to let what sensations are there simply be the sensations there. Sensations at the hands, at the shoulders, in the face – keep these in awareness as you feel the body breathing.

3. Hold all these sensations, together with the sense of the breath and of the body as a whole, in a broad, spacious awareness, simply resting with a gentle attention to the changing field of sensations throughout the body from one moment to the next.

4. As ever, the mind will wander. When it does, just notice where it went – you might want to lightly label that: 'Ah, there's thinking . . .' or 'Oh yes, planning . . .' and then gently and kindly return the attention to the breath and the body as a whole.

5. Keep it all simple – just staying with the changing pattern of sensations throughout the body – from one moment to the next.

6. If you find that you experience sensations that are particularly intense in some part of the body, and that your attention is repeatedly drawn to these sensations – away from the breath or the body as a whole – you could gently shift your posture. Stay aware of the intention to move and of all the sensations involved in the actual movement. Or else you might bring the focus of attention right into the region of greatest intensity and with a gentle attention explore the detailed pattern of sensations there. What, precisely, are the qualities of those sensations? Where, exactly, are they located? Do they vary over time or shift around even with the region of greatest intensity? Just sense what is there, directly experiencing it.

7. You could also explore using the breath to carry your

awareness right into the region of intensity, breathing into it, breathing out from it. Not tensing and bracing, instead opening and softening. As far as you can, just be with whatever's there – allowing, letting it be.

8. And, in the final few minutes of the meditation, bring your attention once more just to the breath. Maybe notice that the breath is always there and it can be an anchor to return to in order to give yourself some calm or balance and some sense of simple self-acceptance.

MINDFULNESS OF SOUNDS AND THOUGHTS MEDITATION

Those who have opted for Stream 1 home practice will now go on to extend their sitting-meditation practice still further. Having started the session of sitting with mindfulness of breathing and then gone straight on to add in a session of mindfulness of the breath and body, you will now continue to sit and add in a session of mindfulness of sounds and thoughts meditation.

In the first part of this meditation you begin by keeping your attention with the breath and the body as a whole, and then you let go of the particular attention to the breath and the body and instead open your attention wide to take in sounds from all directions – just letting sounds come and letting them go. You're not *thinking about* sounds here. Rather, you're simply *experiencing* them. Not thinking about the meanings or implications of sounds, simply allowing them to be patterns of sense experience with their own rhythm, pitch, timbre and duration. Let them come, go and change as they do. Simply let them be.

After a while, you drop that particular attention to sounds and move on to the second part of the practice, turning your attention to what's moving in your mind.

This can be a little trickier. What you will have noticed so far in all the meditation practices you have done is that the mind is rarely still. Thoughts, images, memories, emotions – all of these come and go in the space of the mind. Up till now, whenever you've noticed that some kind of mental activity has pulled your attention away from your intended focus, the instruction has been simply to notice that this has happened, to see where your mind went and then gently bring your attention back to the breath, or the breath and body, or sounds. Now you're going to do something different. Instead of noticing a thought or other kind of mental activity and then letting go of it, the intention here is instead to observe it – to 'let it be' as it changes and flows – and continue to notice, paying attention from moment to moment to whatever is moving in the space of the mind.

This is a subtle practice and here it's even more important than usual to let go of any attempt to 'get it right'. There are a few tricky points to deal with. Firstly, when you turn your attention to thoughts or images or other mental activity, it's very easy to get swept up into them. One moment you may be observing a thought, then very quickly you find yourself *thinking* that thought. That's just how it sometimes goes. It's not a mistake, but see what it's like to come back to that 'observer' perspective, over and over.

There's also sometimes a strange mechanism at work here. When you become mindful of a thought or other mental activity, that very process of mindful attention can take up the mental resources that were involved in that thought or mental activity in the first place. So, whereas previously when you meditated there may have been lots of thoughts, now you might find that when you consciously seek to attend to thoughts there are no thoughts there to be attended to!

This is quite common and it's not a problem. If it happens to you, just gently notice that the thought 'There are no thoughts here' is itself a thought, and continue to observe whatever is moving in the space of the mind – even if there is not very much there at all.

Finally, you may find that, without a definite focus such as the breath or the breath and the body, the mind can become quite agitated in meditation. If that's the case for you, just notice that and, gently and kindly, bring your attention to the breath for a few moments to gain some steadiness before broadening the focus once more.

BOX 5: MINDFULNESS OF SOUNDS AND THOUGHTS

1. As much as you can, keep your attention with the breath, as it moves in and out of the body.
2. Aware of the body as a whole, breathing, begin gently to attend to the field of sensations throughout the body, from one moment to the next.
3. Then, allow the focus of your attention to shift from sensations in the body to hearing. Move your attention to the sense of sound and let that awareness open and expand, becoming receptive to whatever sounds arise.
4. There's no need to go searching for sounds, or to listen out for particular sounds. Instead, simply become receptive to sounds from all directions – aware of obvious sounds and of more subtle sounds, aware of the spaces between sounds, aware of silence.
5. As best you can, stay aware of sounds *as* sounds. Notice any tendency to interpret sounds, to attach stories and meanings to them and, instead, see what it's like to just sit with an awareness of their sensory qualities: their changing pitch, loudness, rhythm and duration.
6. After a time, let go of your awareness of sounds and, instead, open your attention to whatever is moving in

your mind. Just observing – thoughts, images, dreams, emotions . . .

7. Just as sounds are experiences in the mind, so too your thoughts and other mental activity are simply experiences in the mind. And just as sounds arise, remain for a time and then pass, so too thoughts arise, develop and pass.

8. There is no need to try to make thoughts come or go – just let them arise and pass naturally, as they will.

9. Like clouds in the sky, thoughts arise, they drift through the mind and they pass away again. And whether these clouds are dark and stormy or white and feathery, just notice them, letting them be.

10. You may find other analogies helpful here: you might see your thoughts like the carriages of a railway train, passing through a station. But it's not your train. You don't have to get onto it. You can just be content to watch it go by.

11. Or maybe your thoughts are like leaves on a stream, just floating downstream while you're sitting on the bank watching.

12. If any thoughts come to you with intense feelings or emotions, pleasant or unpleasant, as much as you can just note their 'emotional charge' and intensity and simply let them be.

13. If your mind becomes unfocused and scattered, if it gets repeatedly drawn into the drama of your thinking and imagining, perhaps come back to the breath for a few moments, using the breath as an anchor to gently steady your focus.

14. Before bringing the practice to a close, you might spend a few moments coming back to the breath again and following each in-breath and each out-breath.

CHOICELESS AWARENESS

There's not much to be said about this practice. All you do is keep your attention on whatever arises in the space of the mind and body in each passing moment.

The intention here is to stay *present* with whatever arises. Thoughts, emotions, memories, images, sounds, body sensations, impulses . . . Let these come and go as they do and just stay present, resting in present-moment attention to whatever arises.

There is no agenda for this practice apart from embodied wakefulness.

 BOX 6: CHOICELESS AWARENESS

1. Begin by just following the breath for a few moments and then expand that attention to take in the breath and the body.
2. Then, when you're ready, let go of the focus on the breath and allow your field of awareness to open to whatever arises in the landscape of the mind, the body and the world around you. Just being as awake and open as you can be.
3. Letting go of the intention to focus on any particular object, simply rest in awareness, effortlessly apprehending whatever arises from moment to moment. Perhaps the breath, or body sensations, or sounds, thoughts or emotions. Just sitting – completely awake, not holding on to anything, not looking for anything.
4. If the mind becomes too scattered at any time, you might come back to the breath to steady your focus. Then, letting go of attention to the breath again, come back to a state of simple openness.

5. Like an empty mirror, simply reflect whatever comes before it: expecting nothing, clinging to nothing.
6. Awareness itself, attending to the entire field of present-moment experience with stillness.

WORKING THE LENS OF ATTENTION

The meditation practices this week start with a session of focused attention and then go on to broaden the scope of attention. When you're watching a performance on stage, sometimes the lighting technicians narrow the beam of light on the stage so that it picks up just one performer – leaving the rest of the stage in the dark. Sometimes they choose to flood the stage with light, so that you see the whole stage equally. In between these two extremes there are all kinds of ways that the lighting can be adjusted, to allow the audience to focus on more or on less of what's happening on stage.

In the same way, you can work the lens of your own attention. Sometimes you maintain a fairly narrow focus – maybe just attending to the sensations of each breath. Sometimes you maintain a much wider focus – perhaps noticing sounds coming and going. And there are all kinds of other options as well.

There are real benefits to be had from being able to work the lens of your attention. Focused attention can calm and steady the mind. It can help you to stay present in the face of difficult experiences and to reconnect with the present moment when automatic pilot has taken you off into one or another reaction.

A more spacious kind of attention, on the other hand, lets you connect with the broader picture. It allows you to be aware not just of challenging experiences but also of the way in which you are relating to them. That can help you to alter your relationship to difficulty, perhaps by helping you move from an 'avoidance' to an 'approach' mode of mind.

When you come to a more spacious way of attending to your experience, that can help you to counter the way reactions can sometimes bring about a state of contraction, a kind of hard, defensive tightening in the face of difficulty. A more spacious mode of attention can help you to loosen around that, to open, soften and find a bit more ease.

A more spacious mode of attention can help you to see things more broadly. Although there may be difficulty in some parts of your experience it's probably not all-pervasive – there may be parts of your experience that are simply OK. After all, so long as you're breathing there's certainly more right with you than there is wrong with you!

(i) BOX 7: THE NEUROPHYSIOLOGY OF STRESS

About 12,000 years ago our ancestors discovered the possibilities of settled agriculture, and that changed everything. Before then, early humans lived in bands as hunter-gatherers, roaming the forests or the savannah, getting by on what they could kill or forage, living a mode of life that began some 2.6 million years ago.

We've only lived in settled societies for a tiny fraction of the time over which our species has evolved – just over half of 1 per cent of the time. In evolutionary terms, that's pretty close to no time at all. A large part of the biological hardware and software that regulates the ways in which we behave was laid down in much more primitive circumstances, and by understanding how some of it works you can become better able to use it effectively.

Let's go back in time and take a look at the key neurobiological systems that emerged in the very distant past and which have been hugely effective at ensuring our survival as a species.

Imagine that you're out in the forest, hunting or foraging, and you hear a low growl that tells you that there is a bear behind that rock. The wind is blowing towards you, the bear hasn't sniffed you out yet – what happens now?

Millions of years of evolution have gifted you with a set of neurobiological systems that kick in immediately, working together really rapidly to try to ensure your survival. You don't need to think about these – what happens now is pretty much automatic.

What is known as the body's 'sympathetic nervous system' activates. Your amygdalae, parts of the brain connected among other things with fear responses, fire up and a cascade of neurotransmitters such as adrenaline, noradrenalin and cortisol flood your system. Instantly your whole body–mind system is tipped into the 'fight, flight, freeze' mode.

Your muscles tighten and you hold your breath – that keeps you from alerting the bear to your presence. The shot of adrenalin from the glands just above your kidneys causes your heart rate and blood pressure to shoot up, pumping your large muscle groups with blood so you're ready to fight or run away. You stop digesting – you don't want to be wasting energy on digestion if there's a bear behind that rock. Non-essential neural circuits shut down. You don't need to be recalling the exact formulation of Pythagoras' theorem if there's a bear behind that rock – you just want to do what your most basic brain functions allow you to do: fight or run. Cortisol floods your system. This diverts energy from your immune system to deal with the present danger. That undermines your immune response, but if there's a bear behind that rock it doesn't matter that you might get flu next week – that's not your current problem. Cortisol is also an anti-inflammatory, which is great if you're about to be cut or bruised.

So you get away from the bear, return to the family campfire with what you've killed and foraged, and another set of systems kicks in. The 'parasympathetic nervous system' now takes over. The parasympathetic or 'calm and connect' system helps you to recover from the degrading effects of the sympathetic 'flight, flight, freeze' system.

You sit with family and friends, eating and feeling safe. People may be singing, making up songs and dances about your miraculous escape from the bear, and everyone's feeling good. Vasopressin has helped to regulate your heart rate and blood pressure, oxytocin is released and that helps the sense of bonding and social ease. There is an increased secretion of immunoglobulin A and natural-killer-cell production is enhanced, strengthening the immune system. Your hippocampus is stimulated, improving memory and allowing for new learning, and everyone feels fine.

In this state, you're generally likely to experience events as predominantly positive rather than threatening or negative, and that further stimulates the parasympathetic system.

This all works really well if there is a bear that you need to escape from. But it can be positively unhelpful in the kind of environment where most of us experience stressful challenges today.

Take the fear of public speaking. A survey of the US population in 1973 found that fear of speaking before a group was the most commonly reported of all the fears surveyed. In fact it was reported more than twice as often as the fear of death.

Imagine that you have that fear and, to help you overcome it, you decide that you're going to confront it and you volunteer to give a presentation on your favourite hobby to a local shared-interest group. 'Hardly anyone will turn up,' you think to yourself, 'maybe a dozen at most. It will be an easy dry run.' But, arriving at the hall, you see that 50 people have turned up to hear you speak.

What happens now?

Your sympathetic nervous system activates, setting you up to fight, run or freeze. Your heart rate and blood pressure soar, pumping your muscles with blood so you're ready to fight or run away. Your muscles tighten and your breath constricts: you don't want to alert a potential predator to your presence. You stop digesting; your brain shuts down so you can't think clearly; and cortisol floods your system, getting you set up to heal from any cuts or bruising.

This is the legacy of millions of years of evolution, and it's not had time to adapt to the situation you find yourself in today. You can't rely on your evolutionary heritage to help you cope with such challenges. In fact, it often gets in the way.

The good news is that with mindfulness training you can learn to institute conscious threat responses when unconscious threat reactions kick in.

So you arrive at the hall, see a group of expectant faces, feel yourself beginning to get anxious. You notice the sensations of anxiety and do a three-step breathing space to help you to cope. That helps you to calm and get ready for your presentation. There are these fluttering sensations in your stomach, but you turn towards them with mindful attention.

'Gosh, I've got butterflies in my stomach. Hey, butterflies . . . They really *do* feel like butterflies. That's extraordinary.

That's where that saying comes from. Wow – a stomach full of butterflies. That's amazing!'

Letting what is here *be* what is here doesn't immediately eliminate your nervousness, but the act of turning towards the sensations in your stomach with mindful curiosity shifts you into an approach mode of mind and away from an avoidant one.

An avoidant mode of mind narrows the scope of your attention and keeps you stuck in habitual patterns of reactivity. In an approach mode of mind the scope of your attention can broaden – new resources become available and, aware that you're still nervous and that you're allowed to be so, you're now sufficiently resourced to do the presentation well.

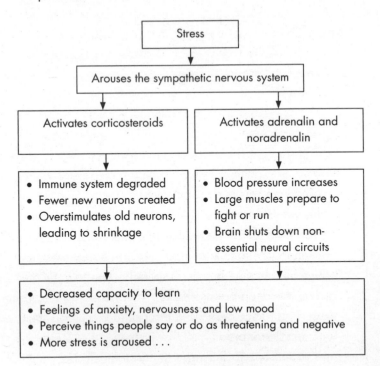

Diagram 1: Sympathetic Nervous System

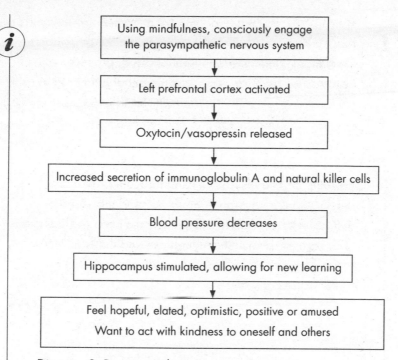

Diagram 2: Parasympathetic Nervous System

Threat reactions are rapid and unconscious. Using your slower conscious resources, you can notice them kicking in and it's at that point, when you become mindful of what is happening, that you can make a change.

Someone cuts in front of you in traffic, your threat reactions kick in and your heart rate soars, your hands tighten on the steering wheel, your shoulders go up and your stomach starts to churn. Then you notice what's going on, become mindful of your body and your breath, take a few deep breaths, soften your hands on the wheel, loosen your shoulders, keep your attention with your breath for a few more breaths and so institute a more effective and more conscious stress-response.

Habitual stress reactivity sensitises the threat-reaction

system. You can begin to live on a bit more of a hair trigger. Regular mindfulness practice, on the other hand, tones that system down. In time and with practice, you become less reactive and more readily able instead to respond.

BOX 8: STREAM 1
HOME PRACTICE FOR WEEK FOUR

- Practise 40 minutes of sitting meditation in a single session of sitting meditation three times this week (⊙14 ⊙40 mins).
- On days when you're not doing 40 minutes of sitting, do 30 minutes of sitting meditation (⊙15 ⊙30 mins) and, either straight after that or at another time, do 10 minutes of walking meditation, using the track 'Walking Meditation' (⊙9 ⊙10 mins) for guidance at least once – after that, try doing it without guidance.
- Practise the three-step breathing space at least three times a day, either when you think of it or connecting it to three regular activities you do or places you go to every day (maybe on waking up and/or going to bed; before a television programme you usually watch; before a particular meal; on first sitting down in your car, or on the bus or at your desk).
- In addition, practise the three-step breathing space whenever you notice unpleasant feelings or come to feel unbalanced.
- Take some time to reflect on these halfway-review questions:
  - What am I learning through this process?
  - What do I need to do over the next four weeks to get the most out of the rest of the course?

BOX 9: STREAM 2
HOME PRACTICE FOR WEEK FOUR

- Practise 20 minutes of sitting meditation at least three times this week (⊙16 ⊙20 mins).
- On the days when you're not doing 20 minutes of sitting meditation, practise the mindfulness of breathing meditation, using the track 'Mindfulness of Breathing (10-Minute Version)' (⊙4 ⊙10 mins), and, either straight afterwards or at another time, do 10 minutes of walking meditation, using the track 'Walking Meditation' (⊙9 ⊙10 mins) for guidance at least once – after that, try doing it without guidance.
- Practise the three-step breathing space at least three times a day, either when you think of it or connecting it to three regular activities you do or places you go to every day (maybe on waking up and/or going to bed; before a television programme you usually watch; before a particular meal; on first sitting down in your car, or on the bus or at your desk.)
- In addition, practise the three-step breathing space whenever you notice unpleasant feelings or come to feel unbalanced.
- Take some time to reflect on these halfway-review questions:
    - What am I learning through this process?
    - What do I need to do over the next four weeks to get the most out of the rest of the course?

WEEK

FIVE

LETTING THINGS BE

Unpleasant and unwanted experiences are an inevitable part of life.

In certain respects you don't have any choice – unpleasant and unwanted experiences *are* inevitable. However you try to set things up, however clever you are about organising yourself and building the life you want for yourself and your loved ones, you'll never eradicate the unwanted. It can't be done. Where you do have a choice, however, is how you respond to the unwanted when it turns up.

As we saw in the previous chapter, there is a natural human tendency to react to the unwanted with aversion. We also saw how mindfulness practice opens up a space of choice. Instead of blindly reacting, it's possible to mindfully respond – and that move from reaction to response can open a gateway onto a path of increasing freedom.

BOX 1: ANOTHER WAY OF BEING WITH WHAT IS DIFFICULT

In the UK these days, border controls at the airports are increasingly stringent and are often understaffed. That means that at busy times the queues there can really build up and seasoned air travellers make a point of learning to work these so they don't have to wait too long.

Sarah was one such passenger. Returning to London from a short trip to Germany, she only had carry-on luggage with her. She'd organised herself a seat near to the front of the plane and as soon as the doors opened she began her dash, walking at a sharp clip to get ahead of the other passengers when they arrived at passport control.

To her dismay, she arrived at the immigration hall to find long lines at each desk. The electronic passport section also wasn't working. 'When will they get that technology sorted?' she muttered inwardly and irritably to herself as she scanned the lines looking for what seemed to be the shortest queue.

Making her choice, she joined a line and stood, waiting, tapping her fingertips against her thigh with barely suppressed impatience.

But she'd not made the smart choice she thought she had. After a few minutes, the official at the desk took someone's passport and walked off for a consultation with his supervisor. No one replaced him at the desk, but all the other lines had by now grown and none were moving very quickly anyway. Sarah was stuck and she began to fume. She turned to the person behind her in the queue: 'This is so incompetent! Look at these lines! What kind of message is this sending to visitors to our country?' But the person behind her didn't want to engage with that and Sarah was left stewing. Her jaw was painfully tight, her shoulders tensed and her stomach was clenched.

Then she remembered something she had heard when she attended a mindfulness taster session that had been offered to people at her work. 'OK,' she thought, 'there's nothing to lose, let's try that now.' She turned her attention to her body, first to the clenched sensation in her stomach.

To her surprise, it was hot there – really intense. It was almost as if she had a kettle boiling inside. 'Gosh,' she thought, 'I'm steaming inside – really steaming!' Standing with that sensation and that image, breathing with it, she found herself increasingly interested in what was happening inside her. It was so complex. There was the feeling of heat, the complex of tensions, the feeling of resistance to those tensions . . .

And then to Sarah's complete astonishment the whole picture changed. In an instant. All that tension dropped away. The heat just vanished, and she stood there, amazed, breathing – waiting patiently in line and wondering at what she'd just experienced.

Sarah turned *towards* what she was experiencing. She paid attention to how her feelings of anger and frustration were showing up in her body, and then those feelings and sensations suddenly vanished. Let's take a closer look at what went on here.

To begin with, the long and unpredictable queues at passport control produced feelings of anger and frustration for Sarah. Those are themselves unpleasant feelings and they gave rise to feelings of aversion – Sarah didn't want to be experiencing them. That set up a feedback loop.

In Sarah's mind – at first anyway – the UK border controls were responsible for her anger and frustration. But she then came to see that it was actually something else altogether. It was her attitude of *avoidance* that was keeping the system in place. So long as she remained unmindful of the aversive system that was feeding and sustaining her anger, it stayed in place. But the moment she switched from an avoidant mode of mind into an *approach* mode of mind, turning towards her experience with interest and curiosity, she stopped fuelling those self-perpetuating loops and the whole situation changed.

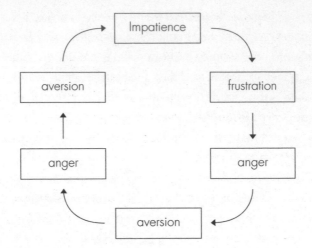

This story illustrates one of the central messages of the mindfulness approaches: it is your relationship to what is difficult or challenging that keeps you stuck in suffering – not the unpleasant feelings and sensations that often come alongside difficulty or challenge.

As we saw earlier, a central aspect of mindfulness is that it calls on us to allow what is the case to be the case. We also saw that this 'allowing' attitude comes alongside another set of attitudes: kindness, gentleness and curiosity. At this stage in the course, I hope you're beginning to get something of a flavour of all these attitudes. The aim of this week's practice is to take all of that one stage further.

ALLOWING: LETTING THINGS BE

This week, the course asks you to begin to experiment with simply allowing difficult or challenging experiences along with the thoughts, feelings, sensations and impulses that come with them, to remain in awareness without trying to change or get rid of them.

This doesn't mean that you're being asked simply to resign yourself to what is difficult. Resignation is quite different. When you're resigned you don't want to be having the experience you're having but you feel quite helpless about changing it, so you just put up with it. 'Allowing and letting things be' is much more active than that. It involves a willingness to experience – an openness to life in all of its complexity. It calls for practice, energy and conscious commitment. Instead of being the passive victim of reactive aversion, the attitude of allowing and letting things be invites you to choose how to respond to difficulty – to approach it with curiosity, kindness and interest.

By holding things gently in awareness – curious and kind – you affirm that in some way you can face what is difficult; that you can name it and work with it.

This radical and powerfully counter-intuitive attitude to difficulty is wonderfully captured by the thirteenth-century Sufi poet Rumi in his poem entitled 'The Guest House'.

BOX 2: THE GUEST HOUSE

This being human is a guest house.
Every morning a new arrival.

A joy, a depression, a meanness,
some momentary awareness comes
as an unexpected visitor.

Welcome and entertain them all!
Even if they are a crowd of sorrows,
who violently sweep your house
empty of its furniture,
still, treat each guest honourably.
He may be clearing you out
for some new delight.

The dark thought, the shame, the malice.
Meet them at the door laughing and invite them in.
Be grateful for whatever comes,
because each has been sent
as a guide from beyond.

Jelaluddin Rumi, translated by Coleman Barks

In Week Four we saw that instead of automatically reacting to stressors you can mindfully respond to them. In order to do that, you need first of all to experience the stressor just as it is, in the present moment. In other words you need to let it be as it is.

This attitude of allowing and letting be is something you can systematically cultivate in practice. To get a sense of how this might work for you more in daily life, try the 'sitting with the difficult' meditation practice in Box 3. The intention of this practice isn't to make things uncomfortable for you. Rather, it's an opportunity to use the 'laboratory conditions' for your mind that you create in meditation to see more clearly how you habitually react to what is difficult and to consciously explore what it might be like to take a more allowing approach.

If you want to try this practice, get set up for meditation and listen to the guidance on Track 17 of the downloads.

Here, you begin with the mindfulness of breathing to establish some degree of calm and focus. You then go on to mindfulness of the breath and body to broaden your field of attention and become more fully aware of what may be going on in your body from moment to moment. In the final section, sitting with the difficult, you begin consciously to explore what it's like to allow whatever difficult or unwanted experiences showed up in your meditation simply to be as they are. As much as you can, bring an attitude of gentle and kindly curiosity to those experiences: allowing them, letting them be. In particular, in this practice you might discover that turning *towards* any body sensations that are present at a time of difficulty can be really helpful. If the body sensations are themselves the source of difficulty, such as a chronic pain, moving your attention right into that area with an attitude of gentle and kindly curiosity might help you to change your relationship to the pain and the way you experience it. If your difficulty is more in the area of thoughts and feelings, then turning towards any body sensations that show up at that time changes the focus of your attention – it can help you to avoid any tendency to rumination, for example, or repeatedly turning anxious thoughts over in your mind.

BOX 3: 'SITTING WITH THE DIFFICULT' MEDITATION

1. Begin by practising a session of mindfulness of breathing followed by mindfulness of the breath and body.

2. Then, scan through the different elements of your experience right now. What thoughts are here? What feelings, sensations and impulses – if any? Gently acknowledge these, noticing them with no particular attempt to change them. You're not trying to move your attention away from these right now, or to make them in any way other than they are.

3. Then, if any of these thoughts, feelings, sensations or impulses feel in any way challenging or unwanted, see what it's like to be with these differently – allowing, letting them be.

4. If you find challenging thoughts or feelings in the moment, you might take a look and see what body sensations or impulses come along with these. Or if you're encountering unwanted sensations in the body, take a look and see what thoughts, feelings and impulses come along.

5. You may find connections here or you may not. It's not important to *think* about that – rather the intention here is simply to notice, to see what's here and allow it to be so.

6. If you encounter unwanted body sensations, you might explore moving your attention right into the heart of the sensation – approaching, rather than avoiding, what is difficult.

7. You might experiment with 'breathing into' the sensation, 'breathing out' from it, approaching this imaginatively – just as you did in the body scan.

8. See what it's like to keep your attention focused on the physical aspect of what is unwanted. As best you can, keep your attention on that part of the body where the sensations are strongest, holding what you find there with a gesture of welcoming: curious, kind, allowing. This isn't a cold and clinical investigation, it's gentle, warm and kind.

9. Whatever shows up – whatever feelings, sensations, thoughts or impulses – they're all allowed. These are the guests in your guest house, coming and going. See what it's like to treat them honourably, with warmth and kindness.

10. Keep noticing, watching sensations shifting, noticing their changing intensity.

11. When your attention settles for a time and you're able to stay with the changing flow of sensations for a while, you might try deepening your allowing attitude. You could, for instance, say in your mind, 'It's OK – I can be with this. Here it is. It's allowed. Let me be open to it.' Or any other set of phrases that works for you. Not tensing or bracing against unwanted sensations, instead opening and softening. If it helps, on the out-breath you might say to yourself 'opening', 'softening' over and over.

12. Remember that by saying, 'It's OK – I can be with this . . .' or 'It's allowed . . . 'you're not saying that everything's fine. You're not pretending. You're simply staying open to what's here, letting what *is* the case *be* the case. You might even inwardly say to yourself, 'It's OK not to want these feelings and sensations, but here they are. Let me be open to them.'

13. You don't have to *like* what you're experiencing right now. But see what it's like to stay with it – allowing, letting it be.

14. Remember, not all unwanted physical sensations come with a strong emotional charge. If you don't find any strong emotions as you're sitting through this practice that's fine – just stay with whatever body sensations turn up – especially those that aren't pleasant.

Try doing a version of this practice in your daily life. As you're going about your day, see what it's like to bring an attitude of gentle and kindly curiosity to whatever thoughts, feelings, sensations or impulses your mind is repeatedly drawn towards. Take a moment to notice how you relate to what arises there.

When you do this, you might notice that sometimes you experience your thoughts, feelings, sensations and so on in a non-accepting, reactive way. It's part of the human condition to try to hold on to those experiences you like, becoming attached. Or to push away experiences you don't like – out of fear, irritation or annoyance, tightening and contracting in the face of these.

Allowing and letting your experience be means making space for whatever is going on rather than trying to create some other state. That lets you settle into an awareness of what is present.

The easiest way to relax is to stop trying to make things different.

But the allowing approach we're discussing here isn't a clever way of 'fixing' your experience or getting rid of the unwanted. This isn't about trying deliberately to change your feelings – that would be avoidant. Instead, the intention here is to soften the way unwanted experiences are held in awareness: to ease and to open out the relationship of aversion to certain experiences that underlies so much of our distress. Sometimes the feelings or sensations may change, sometimes they may not. The main thing you're trying to do here is to change how you *relate* to them – and that changes everything.

As we've seen, acceptance is *not* resignation. Rather, it allows you, as a vital first step, to become fully aware of difficulties and to respond in a skilful way rather than reacting in kneejerk fashion by automatically running the familiar unhelpful strategies you might have for dealing with them.

TREAT YOURSELF WITH KINDNESS

At the heart of the 'allowing' approach we've been discussing is a background attitude of friendliness and kindness towards your own experience.

As we saw in Week Two, you set out to do all the practices on this course with the intention of paying attention to your experience with an attitude of gentle kindliness towards whatever arises. You may recall that I drew attention to three key terms in that chapter: intention, attention and attitude. We saw how in the course of practising we tend to forget and remember all three of these. Over and over.

Over and over you forget and then remember to bring an attitude of gentle kindliness to whatever it is that you're experiencing as you practise. By doing that, very gradually, a greater capacity for gentleness and kindness towards your experience might emerge.

BOX 4: RELATING TO AVERSION

My friend and colleague John Teasdale, one of the founders of MBCT, once wrote in a paper that he and I published about how once he found himself on a training course, preparing to give a talk on the way in which craving and aversion drive human suffering.

'Experience itself is not the problem,' he planned to tell his audience, 'the problem is our relationship to it – our need to have it be a particular way.'

Turning these thoughts over in his mind as he woke in the night before he was due to give that talk, he realised, with mild annoyance, that he had become quite awake. His mind's immediate reaction was, 'Oh no, I don't want to be lying here awake for hours, I have to find a way to get back to sleep.' So, even though his thinking had just been focused on the idea that the problem is not experience itself, but our relationship to it, his immediate reaction was to try to work out how to be rid of this unwanted wakefulness, rather than to look at how he was relating to it.

But because he had been thinking about what he planned say about craving, aversion and human suffering, it wasn't long before it dawned on him. 'Oh, this is aversion – the problem here is my need not to be awake rather than the wakefulness itself.'

Guided by his memory of that teaching, he then looked more closely at his actual experience, and sensed very clearly in the moment that it was his irritation with being awake, and the somewhat driven quality of his need to get back to sleep, that was the source of his annoyance and, ironically, the main thing keeping him awake. From that clear realisation, there flowed very naturally a letting go of the irritation and of the need to sort out the wakefulness. He consciously befriended his wakefulness, and within a minute or two was back asleep.

As this little story illustrates, if ideas like these can be kept fresh and alive in your mind so that they are available to mould and shape the lens through which you actually see and are aware of difficult experiences, then that can be a vital component in your capacity to transform your suffering.

BOX 5: USING THE THREE-STEP BREATHING SPACE TO COPE WITH DIFFICULTIES

When you are troubled by difficult thoughts, feelings, sensations or impulses you can use the three-step breathing space to help you to cope.

1. As we saw in Week Three, you begin the breathing space by deliberately adopting an upright, dignified posture, and bringing attention to your experience in the present moment. When using the breathing space to cope with a difficulty, you pay particular attention to whatever difficult experience has shown up, acknowledging and identifying it. You might try putting the experience into words. For instance, you could inwardly say, 'Feelings of anger are arising . . .' or 'Self-critical thoughts are here . . .' or 'Pain is here . . .' These simple acknowledgements are an important first step in allowing your experience to be your experience.
2. Then, gently focus your full attention on the breath. As best you can, fully experience each in-breath and each

out-breath – one after another. The breath can be an anchor here, bringing you into the present and helping you tune in to a state of awareness and stillness. You don't use the breath as an avoidance mechanism here, as a way of tuning out of the difficulty. Rather, you use it to gently sharpen your focus, increasing your capacity for calm and a kindly awareness.

3. Finally, expand that awareness around the breath to the body as a whole, feeling the space it occupies, sensing the whole body breathing. You might also take the breath to any discomfort, tension or resistance you experience, 'breathing in' to the sensations and, while breathing out, allowing them to soften and open. If it helps you could try saying to yourself, 'It's OK to feel what I'm feeling' or 'It's OK not to feel OK.' In this way, simply allow things to be, just as they already are.

Maintaining a sense of the space within and around yourself, hold everything in awareness, to whatever extent you can, and bring this quality of expanded awareness to the next moments of your day.

Practising like this might let you hold difficult experiences in a wider field of awareness when you notice them: letting them be rather than engaging in battle with them.

This 'coping' breathing space can give you a way of stepping out of automatic-pilot mode when dealing with difficulties, reconnecting with the present moment and your own innate wisdom.

BOX 6: STREAM 1
HOME PRACTICE FOR WEEK FIVE

1. Practise the 'sitting with difficulty' meditation once or twice this week – using track ⬇17 (⏱30 mins) for guidance.

2. For your regular practice, do a 40-minute meditation using track ⬇14 (⏱40 mins) for guidance. If you'd like to, you might try a few sessions of sitting without audio guidance. If you want to keep to time and have a smartphone, there are several apps available specifically to help with this in the context of meditation. I use Insight Timer myself – but do look around and choose your own.

3. Practise the three-step breathing space three times each day. You could either do this when you think of it or you could connect it to three regular activities you do or places you go to, such as on first waking up or before going to bed, before a television programme you regularly watch, before a meal, on first sitting down in your car or on the bus or train, or when you get to your desk or other workstation.

4. Whenever you notice yourself starting to feel stressed, practise the three-step breathing space to cope, exploring ways of responding with greater mindfulness and more friendliness to yourself and the situation.

5. Bring awareness to moments of reaction and explore options for responding with greater mindfulness and creativity. Practise opening up space for responding in the present moment. Explore how using the breath can bring you into the present moment.

6. When you find yourself willing to 'embrace the unwanted', what does that feel like?

BOX 7: STREAM 2
HOME PRACTICE FOR WEEK FIVE

1. Practise a 20-minute 'sitting with difficulty' meditation once this week – using track ⬇18 (◔20 mins) for guidance.
2. For your regular practice, do a 20-minute meditation, either using track ⬇16 (◔20 mins) or any other combination of 10-minute meditations that you'd like to work with. If you'd like to, you might try a few sessions of sitting without audio guidance. If you want to keep to time and have a smartphone, there are several apps available to help with this. I use Insight Timer myself – but do look around and choose your own.
3. Practise the three-step breathing space three times each day. You could either do this when you think of it or you could connect it to three regular activities you do or places you go to, such as on first waking up or before going to bed, before a television programme you regularly watch, before a meal, on first sitting down in your car or on the bus or train, or when you get to your desk or other workstation.
4. Whenever you notice yourself starting to feel stressed, practise the three-step breathing space to cope, exploring ways of responding with greater mindfulness and more friendliness to yourself and the situation.
5. Bring awareness to moments of reaction and explore options for responding with greater mindfulness and creativity. Practise opening up space for responding in the present moment. Explore how using the breath can bring you into the present moment.
6. When you find yourself willing to 'embrace the unwanted', what does that feel like?

WEEK

SIX

RECOGNISING THOUGHTS AND EMOTIONS AS MENTAL EVENTS

MAKING MEANING

What you think can have powerful effects on how you feel and what you do.

As you'll have noticed by now in your meditation, once triggered, thoughts can then run on automatically. In your meditation you'll have been becoming aware, over and over again, of the thoughts and images passing through the mind.

Letting go of thoughts and returning your attention to the breath and the present moment, over and over, you may now be beginning to get some capacity to distance yourself from them. Even just the smallest paper-thin distance can let you begin to get some perspective on your thoughts so you can start to see that they are just mental events. They are not truth, reality or 'me'. Thoughts are just thoughts. When you see that, it can allow you to see that there may be other ways to think about things and this can free you from the tyranny of unhelpful thought patterns.

The thoughts and images that come to you over and again can sometimes give you an indication of what's going on deeper in the mind. It may be possible to get hold of them and look them over from a number of different perspectives. By becoming more familiar with your habitual, automatic, unhelpful thinking patterns you can become more aware of, and change, the processes that lead you into less resourceful ways of thinking and feeling.

Consider this little scenario:

John was on his way to school.
He was worried about the maths lesson.
He didn't think he could control the class today.
After all, it wasn't part of a caretaker's duty.

Notice what happens here. Out of tiny scraps of information you build a picture. Line by line, each reader will construct their own picture.

'John was on his way to school.'

Maybe you see a little schoolboy with a book bag, skipping happily along.

'He was worried about the maths lesson.'

Oh dear – the image changes and you might even feel a burst of empathy for his anxiety and imagine the anxious set of his shoulder, the tiny furrow in his brow.

'He didn't think he could control the class today.'

Whoops! He's a teacher. OK – maybe the image of a new teacher comes to mind, somewhat anxious, still learning the job.

'It wasn't part of a caretaker's duty.'

Aha! You might chuckle to yourself as you see the little trap the scenario set for you.

What's particularly interesting here is that, until the scenario sprang its little trap, it's very unlikely that you'd have been aware of what you were doing – that you were making meaning as you went along. It's just what we humans do. It's how we get by in the world. It's neither right nor wrong, but it can get us into trouble.

We make meaning out of tiny scraps of information, and the meanings we make almost always go well beyond the facts we're given. We constantly update our picture of the world as new information becomes available – just as you did when you read through that scenario. But, until the world plays a trick on us, as that scenario did, we're very unlikely to be aware of the fact that it's actually we ourselves who are making that meaning. By and large we think that we're seeing the world as it actually is.

Mindfulness training can make a powerful difference here.

Think about what's been happening in your meditation practice so far. Say you're doing a session of mindfulness of breathing meditation. You set out to follow your breath; then you start to think and for a time you become lost in thought; then you realise that you're thinking; you let go of the thought and you bring your attention back to the breath. If you've been doing your home practice with any regularity, by this stage of the course you will have been making those moves hundreds, or more probably thousands, of times. Over and over. You see that you're thinking, you choose not to be thinking and you come back to the breath for one breath . . . two breaths . . . three breaths . . . and you find yourself thinking . . . you choose not to be thinking . . . you come back to the breath. Over and over.

By doing that again and again you're learning to recognise *that* you're thinking *when* you're thinking, and this is not such a common skill. Much of the time most people go about their business without knowing what they're doing in that regard. By and large, most people think without knowing that they're thinking. That's fine, it generally works, but it can sometimes create problems.

OUR MOODS AND FEELINGS COLOUR OUR THOUGHTS

Consider another two very brief scenarios now, outlined below. If you can, read Scenario 1 first and then very briefly consider the thoughts and feelings that come to you as you imagine yourself in those or similar circumstances. Try not to read Scenario 2 until you've done that.

This isn't a trick, and there are no right or wrong answers here. Just be as truthful and reflective as you can be as you consider both scenarios.

Scenario 1

You're feeling low because you've just had an argument with a colleague at work. Shortly afterwards another colleague rushes past you in the corridor saying he or she can't stop.

What might you think? What might you feel?

Consider that briefly before reading on.

Scenario 2

You're feeling happy because you've been praised for some work you did well. Shortly afterwards another colleague rushes past you in the corridor saying he or she can't stop.

What might you think? What might you feel?

Consider that briefly before reading on.

Discussion

Everyone will have their own response to these two scenarios. When we do this exercise on our public courses a few people in each class will say that they respond exactly the same to both scenarios. Others may say things like this:

In the first scenario I thought, 'Oh yes, he's heard about the argument and he's taking sides.' I felt a bit down and slightly angry with him. In the second scenario I thought that maybe he had an important meeting to go to and I hoped he'd be OK.

or

In the first scenario I couldn't imagine why she was ignoring me. I thought, 'Well, you're really on your own here. No one cares . . .' and I felt quite lonely. In the second one I thought maybe she was jealous, but I felt OK with that – that's just how it goes.

And so on. The way we see things and the way we react to them are shaped by the frame of mind we bring to the experience.

When you're in a low frame of mind you see things one way ('he's taking sides'); when you're in a more buoyant frame of mind you see things in another way ('he was in a rush'). In either case your frame of mind shapes the way you interpret the event. The process of making an interpretation is completely natural – it's how we're set up. All we know from the two scenarios outlined above is that a colleague rushes past you in the corridor saying he or she can't stop, but it's very rare to sit with that fact without making *some* kind of interpretation, and generally people don't know *that* they're interpreting *when* they're interpreting.

This diagram shows how experiences like the one described in the above scenarios usually play out.

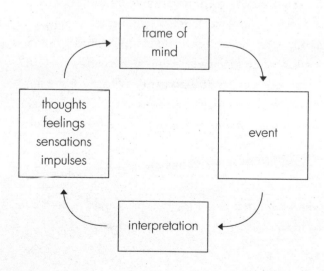

The frame of mind that we bring to an event colours the way we interpret that event and that gives rise to various thoughts, feelings, sensation and impulses which in turn colour our frame of mind. Our interpretations of events reflect what we bring to those events, as much as – or sometimes even more than – what is actually there. We always see the world through one or another lens and that in turn shapes our thinking and our feeling.

What is more, when you're in one or another mood, the thinking patterns that emerge from that will often echo the elements that shaped that mood in the first place. When you're feeling hopeless you'll tend to have hopeless thoughts; when you're feeling kind you'll tend to have benevolent thoughts. That process establishes a kind of bias whereby feelings shape thoughts and thoughts confirm feelings.

BOX 1: MINDFULNESS AND MENTAL PROLIFERATION

'Mental proliferation' translates a term that was used in the ancient psychological tradition that developed alongside mindfulness in Asia. It refers, among other things, to the mind's tendency to fabricate meaning and create elaborate scenarios out of very little.

Perhaps you've had an experience a bit like this. You come into a room and everyone in it falls silent. You can then go off on long processes of mental proliferation, developing complex scenarios to explain why that happened: 'They don't like me and they were talking about me and it's all because of what happened yesterday when I . . . and then I . . . but she should never have . . . so from now on I'll just . . .' and so on.

But maybe all that happened is that there was a pause in the conversation.

Very often, such proliferations are pure fiction. They're fabrications, a process of mental elaboration that proceeds from the uncomfortable feeling of not knowing what was going on when you came into the room. In response to a tiny moment of discomfort, a process of elaboration is set in train, little of which bears any relation to simple, present-moment reality.

In order to exit from these elaborative processes and stay with present-moment reality, it can help to turn to your sense of the body, here and now. Yes, it may be uncomfortable to enter a room where everyone falls silent. Where in the body do you feel that discomfort? Does it shift and change over time? How widely in the body do you feel it? If you can tune in to that, then you ground yourself in present-moment reality – the experience of discomfort – without leaping off into ungrounded abstractions that 'explain' and justify the discomfort. It's just uncomfortable – full stop.

Mindfulness training really helps here. When uncomfortable feelings arise, or when you find yourself caught up in a process of mental proliferation, if you've been doing your meditation practice regularly you may find yourself that bit more able to exercise choice. Acknowledging the thoughts you're having, you might choose to attend to something else instead. Rather than feeding the process, you might, for example, take your attention to the breath for a time and use the breath to anchor your awareness in your body. That can bring you back to present-moment, here-and-now reality.

When you know that your thoughts are just thoughts

and that they're not facts – even the ones that say they are – it can be really liberating.

BOX 2: MINDFULLY RELATING TO THOUGHTS

In the Introduction, we saw how MBCT came to be developed out of MBSR partly as a result of what its founders saw when they read a passage from Jon Kabat-Zinn's *Full Catastrophe Living*. That passage is particularly pertinent to this week's theme. Here it is in full:

> It is remarkable how liberating it feels to be able to see that your thoughts are just thoughts and that they are not 'you' or 'reality'. For instance, if you have the thought that you must get a certain number of things done today and you don't recognize it as a thought, but act as if it's 'the truth', then you have created a reality *in that moment* in which you really believe that those things must all be done today.
>
> One [MBSR] course participant, Peter, who'd had a heart attack and wanted to prevent another one, came to a dramatic realization of this one night when he found himself washing his car at ten o'clock at night with the floodlights on in the driveway. It struck him that he didn't *have* to be doing this. It was just the inevitable result of a whole day spent trying to fit everything in that he *thought* needed doing. As he saw what he was doing to himself he also saw that he had been unable to question the truth of his original conviction that everything had to get done today, because he was already so completely caught up in believing it.

If you find yourself behaving in similar ways, it is likely that you will also feel driven, tense and anxious without even knowing why, just as Peter did. So if the thought of how much you have to get done today comes up while you are meditating, you will have to be very attentive to it *as a thought* or you may be up and doing things before you know it, without any awareness that you decided to stop sitting simply because a thought came through your mind.

On the other hand, when such a thought comes up, if you are able to step back from it and see it clearly, then you will be able to prioritize things and make sensible decisions about what really does need doing. You will know when to call it quits during the day, and when to take breaks while you are working so you can restore yourself and work most effectively. So the simple act of recognizing your thoughts as *thoughts* can free you from the distorted reality they often create and allow for more clear-sightedness and a greater sense of manageability in your life.

This liberation from the tyranny of the thinking mind comes directly out of the meditation practice itself. When we spend some time each day in nondoing, observing the flow of the breath and the activity of our mind and body, without getting caught up in that activity, we are cultivating calmness and mindfulness hand in hand. As the mind develops stability and is less caught up in the content of thinking, we strengthen the mind's ability to concentrate and to be calm. Each time we recognize a thought as a thought when it arises and we register its content and discern the strength of its hold on us as well as the accuracy of its content, then we let go of it and come back to our breathing and a sense of our body, we are strengthening the mindfulness muscle. In the process we are coming to know ourselves better and becoming more accepting of ourselves, not as we would like to be but as we actually are. This is an expression of our innate wisdom and compassion.

BOX 3: THE COOKIE THIEF: A PARABLE

The writer Valerie Cox tells about a woman who was waiting at an airport one night. With several long hours to go before her flight, she bought a book and a bag of cookies, and found a place where she could sit and read.

Deeply engrossed in the book, she suddenly realised that the man sitting beside her was taking cookies from the bag that was sitting between them. Not wanting to make a scene, she tried to ignore him. But it didn't stop with just one or two cookies – it went on and on. She read and ate and the man continued to eat too. She kept on trying to ignore the situation but found she just got angrier and angrier.

Finally, there was only one cookie left. The man took the last cookie, broke it in half and, with a smile on his face, offered her one half while he ate the other. She took it grudgingly, angrily thinking about how rude he was.

She was about to say something but her flight was called. Gathering her belongings, she headed for the gate, refusing to look back at the 'cookie thief'. Fuming inwardly, she boarded the plane and kept on with her reading.

In the middle of the flight, she reached into her bag and found an unopened pack of cookies inside it.

'If these are mine,' she realised, 'then the cookies we were eating were his! And he tried to share them with me . . .' To her shock and dismay she realised that she'd been the rude one there as well as the thief.

WORKING WITH THOUGHTS
IN MEDITATION

By this stage of the course I hope you'll have come to see that there is more to the mind than thinking. You can attend to sensations, perhaps, or to feelings, without actually thinking about them. You just experience them. And sometimes, even if only for a few seconds, the mind might have calmed to a point where you're not aware of any thoughts at all.

But that's not our usual mode of experience. Most of the time we spend our lives actively engaged with the thinking part of the mind and that habit is so deep that, even though meditation doesn't actually require discursive thought, it often comes along and sweeps your mind away.

The meditation teacher Joseph Goldstein uses the analogy of a train to describe this process. Sometimes you hop onto a train of association, not knowing that you have hopped on, and not knowing the likely destination. Then, some way down the track you wake up and realise that you've been thinking and that you've been taken for a ride. Then you may find that you step down from the train in a very different mental environment from where you hopped aboard.

But meditation is not thought and, through a process of quiet observation, new kinds of understanding can emerge when you meditate. You don't need to fight with thoughts, suppress them or judge them. Rather you can simply choose not to follow thoughts once you become aware that they've arisen.

Right now, take a few moments to look at the thoughts arising and passing in your mind. You might imagine yourself sitting in a cinema watching an empty screen, just waiting for thoughts to arise.

It's likely that they'll show up pretty quickly. But what exactly are they? What happens to them? Where do they come from? Where do they go? They're like magic displays that seem real when we're lost in them but vanish when we look more closely.

And yet these ephemeral phenomena can have so much power. 'Do this, say that, remember, plan, obsess, judge.' Your thoughts have the potential to drive you crazy.

The kinds of thoughts you have and the way they can impact on your life depend in part on your understanding of things. When you can see thoughts arise and pass, just observing the process, then it doesn't really matter what kinds of thoughts appear in your mind. You can begin to see your thoughts as the passing show they really are.

So when you become aware that thoughts have arisen in your meditation, do your best not to judge them and not to react. Just notice and let go, over and over and over. And if your attention wanders hundreds of times, just let go hundreds of times. Sometimes there can be very few thoughts, sometimes it can seem like a swirling maelstrom. The key thing is simply to see what's actually going on. They're just thoughts.

i BOX 4: SO WHY *DON'T* ZEBRAS GET ULCERS?

In 1994, the Stanford University biologist Robert Sapolsky published a book called *Why Zebras Don't Get Ulcers*, an investigation of how stressors are experienced differently by humans and by animals in the wild. Sapolsky wrote his book before it was widely known that peptic ulcers are caused not by stress, coffee consumption or spicy foods, as previously thought, but that about 60 per cent of them are actually caused by a bacterial infection that can fairly easily be cured.

Still, Sapolsky's question is a great one – why don't zebras and other animals get stressed the way we do? Let's have a look at that question from a mindfulness perspective.

Imagine there is a herd of zebra grazing somewhere out on the high grass plains in southern Africa and a pride of lions turns up and begins to stalk them. As soon as they notice the lions, the zebras become highly activated. Some of the neurobiological processes that we share with them spark up in the presence of danger. Their heart rates soar and they start to run.

I'm told, although I've not been able to verify this, that at such times zebras may also engage in unfriendly escape strategies: they may try to trip one another up, or bite a faster zebra's tail to slow them down. 'Rather the lioness gets him than she gets me!' Whatever the truth of that, they're fully focused on escaping the danger.

Eventually the lions will bring down a zebra, kill it and start to eat. And at that moment, all the surviving zebras calm down. The threat has passed. Lions only kill to eat, so once they have killed and are eating they are no longer an active threat. The zebras can then get back to doing what they most want to do – eating grass.

But it's not like that for us. That's partly because, unlike zebras, we're endowed with a wonderfully developed neocortex that enables us to imagine and to abstract. An unfortunate by-product of that wonderful gift is that we can imagine and have abstract thoughts about danger, threats and other stressors long after they actually passed.

If a zebra were more like one of us, here's how its thinking might now go: 'Phew. Great. Got away. That's great . . . But god, look, poor Stripey, they're eating him. Oh my god, they're eating him! That's awful. I didn't know him so well but, hey, you can't know everyone in the herd. He seemed like a nice guy. Really nice. And they're eating him! Maybe I shouldn't have tripped him . . . But if I didn't trip him it would have been me! He'd have tripped me, I know he would . . . So what to do now? I can't stay here, there are lions! I know they say that lions aren't dangerous when they're eating, but – they're lions! Oh no . . . I love the grass here so much. It's so juicy and succulent. But I can't stay here, there are lions! And if I can't eat here, where will I be able to eat? The grass in other parts of the plain isn't as tasty as this grass . . . But no, I can't stay, there are lions. And you know what, that could have been me. I could be lying there, just like Stripey. Oh my god – that could have been me! I can't stay here . . . But if I can't stay here, where can I go? The lions can come anywhere. Oh no . . .' And so on.

Our capacity for abstract thought and imagination allows us to maintain and pursue unresourceful patterns of thought like this well after the stressor that initially gave rise to them has passed. What is more, our biological systems respond to those thoughts and imaginings in pretty much the same way as they do to any other stressor. Thinking like this keeps our 'fight, flight, freeze' system activated. Zebras calm once an active threat passes; humans can keep them imaginatively present for very much longer.

With a bit of mindfulness practice, it becomes easier to spot such unresourceful thinking for what it is. They're just thoughts, just feelings, just imaginings.

THREE STRATEGIES FOR
DEALING WITH DISTRESS

Imagine that a work colleague phones you at 9.30 p.m. in the evening, intruding into your personal time for rest. He wants to talk about some figures you've both been working on. His tone seems accusatory – hectoring. You don't contact work colleagues after 7 p.m., but he just keeps doing it! Angry that your home life has been invaded in that way, after the call, you find yourself upset and irritable, continuously dwelling on the thoughts about the call and your colleague that forced their way into your mind.

Participants in mindfulness-based programmes often report a reduction in distress following events like this. They might describe noticing that, as a result of practising mindfulness, a 'difficult' phone call, which previously might have upset them for hours, now only leads to disturbance and dwelling on the experience for a matter of minutes, or even seconds.

How does this happen? Perhaps because, consciously or not, they have implemented one or another of three strategies for dealing with distress.

The first, and simplest, strategy for altering the conditions which sustain or create suffering is to change the *content* the mind is processing. You can do this by intentionally redirecting the focus of your attention to aspects of experience less likely to support the arising and continuation of configurations that create suffering. So, in the case of the phone call, you might intentionally focus and sustain your attention on the bodily sensations as the breath moves in and out. This relatively neutral focus will provide less 'fuel' for sustaining distress than would the emotion-laden thoughts related to the call.

A second approach is to leave the 'input' to the mind the same, but to change the configuration of processes, or 'shape' of the mind, through which that material is processed. The first strategy changes *what* is processed, this second strategy changes *how* thoughts and feelings are processed. This might mean, for example, intentionally allowing and attending to the unpleasant feelings created by the upsetting phone call with interest and curiosity, as objects of experience, rather than being 'lost' *within* them in the automatic reaction of aversion.

The third strategy is to change the *view* that you have of the material being processed. With the upsetting phone call, this might involve a change from the perception 'That person has really hurt me by the way he spoke' to the perception 'Unpleasant thoughts, feelings and body sensations are here in this moment.' With this strategy you remember that thoughts and feelings are just thoughts and feelings. They come, they go. You witness them without being caught up by them.

Each of these three strategies calls on you to be mindful and aware. If you want to make intentional changes to what is processed, how it is processed or the view you have of it, you need to know what is going on in the moment. The practice of mindfulness cultivates meta-awareness – the capacity to know, directly, intuitively, your experience as it arises in each moment.

BOX 5: UNHELPFUL PATTERNS OF THOUGHT

In Week One, we saw that there are any number of automatic mental routines that can run off without our being aware of them and that some of these can be really unhelpful. They're more likely to occur when you're stressed or anxious, experiencing low mood or in pain. In becoming aware of them and by recognising them for what they are you may find that you have more freedom –

that you can stop identifying with them or taking them at face value. You may find that you can come to see them as 'just thoughts'.

Reflect on the list below. You might want to add some of your own favourites to it:

- **Mind-reading:** 'He thinks I'm stupid/boring/unattractive.'
- **Crystal-ball gazing:** 'I'm not going to enjoy this.'
- **Overestimating the negative:** 'This is going to be a total disaster.'
- **Eternalising:** 'I'll never manage this.' 'I'll always feel like this.'
- **Expecting perfection:** 'I/people shouldn't ever make mistakes.'
- **Overgeneralising:** 'This is difficult – everything's such an effort.'
- **Judgementalism:** 'I wasn't able to do that – I'm just not good enough.'
- **Taking the blame:** 'When things go wrong, it's always my fault.'
- **Laying the blame:** 'When things go wrong, it's always other people's fault.'

BOX 6: USING THE BREATHING SPACE TO WORK WITH THOUGHTS

At the end of the breathing space, if you're still troubled by difficult thoughts, here are some of the things you can do:

- Watch them come and go without feeling that you have to follow them.
- See your thoughts as mental events rather than as facts. It

may be true that a particular mental event often occurs with other feelings and it may be tempting to think of it as being true. But it is still up to you to decide whether it is true and how you want to deal with it.

- Write your thoughts down. This can let you see them in a way which is less emotional and overwhelming. The pause between having the thought and writing it down can give you a moment to reflect on its meaning.
- For particularly difficult thoughts, it may be helpful intentionally to take another look at them later in a balanced open state of mind, as part of your sitting practice – let the wiser part of your mind give its perspective.

BOX 7: STREAM 1
HOME PRACTICE FOR WEEK SIX

1. Do 40 minutes of meditation each day, using track ⬇14 (◉40 mins). If you'd like to, you might try a few sessions of sitting without audio guidance.
2. Practise the three-step breathing space three times each day. You could either do this when you think of it or you could connect it to three regular activities you do or places you go to, such as on first waking up or before going to bed, before a television programme you regularly watch, before a meal, on first sitting down in your car or on the bus or train, or when you get to your desk or other workstation.
3. Notice how you are relating to your thoughts day to day, as well as in the meditation practice.

BOX 8: STREAM 2
HOME PRACTICE FOR WEEK SIX

1. Do 20 minutes of meditation each day, using track ⊙16 (⊕20 mins). If you'd like to, you might try a few sessions of sitting without audio guidance.
2. Practise the three-step breathing space three times each day. You could either do this when you think of it or you could connect it to three regular activities you do or places you go to, such as on first waking up or before going to bed, before a television programme you regularly watch, before a meal, on first sitting down in your car or on the bus or train, or when you get to your desk or other workstation.
3. Notice how you are relating to your thoughts day to day, as well as in the meditation practice.

WEEK

SEVEN

TAKING GOOD CARE OF YOURSELF

By now I hope you will have seen that there are a number of things you can actively do to keep yourself in better shape as you go through the day. Maybe you've already noticed how, by being a bit more mindful in each moment, you can come to make smarter decisions about what you really need in each moment, decisions that are informed by a clearer sense of your own thoughts, feelings, body sensations and impulses from moment to moment.

When you give mindful attention to your own changing experience, you are in a better position to regulate your own mode of mind and you can take better care of your body as well. For example, one of the simplest ways to take care of your physical and mental well-being is to take regular daily exercise: a regular brisk walk, for example, or swimming, jogging, going to the gym, yoga, Pilates, t'ai chi or mindful stretching.

Remember the exhaustion funnel we looked at in Week Four (*see page 158*)? We saw then how, when feeling really pressed at times of stress or other difficulty, we're also likely to begin to give up on the things on the left-hand side of the funnel that actually make our lives sustainable. As these progressively fall away we can move closer and closer to burnout, to a stressed way of life that can't be sustained. Sometimes, maybe often, we just don't take good care of ourselves. Sometimes, maybe often, we can even be a bit unkind to ourselves.

But it doesn't have to be like that. By this stage of the course,

I hope you'll have begun to get a deeper sense of the non-judgemental aspect of mindfulness. Remember the connotations of the word 'judgemental' that we looked at in the Introduction. When you're judgemental you can be critical, hypercritical, condemnatory, negative, disapproving, disparaging or pejorative. Often, the person we're most judgemental about is ourselves.

Becoming more mindful doesn't only mean that you stop judging yourself so harshly and you leave it at that. When you're mindful, that judgementalism is replaced not by a cool, neutral state but actually by something warmer and kinder. As the mindfulness teacher Christina Feldman puts it:

> The quality of mindfulness is not a neutral or blank presence. True mindfulness is imbued with warmth, compassion, and interest. In the light of this engaged attention we discover it is impossible to hate or fear anything . . . that we truly understand. The nature of mindfulness is engagement; where there is interest, a natural, unforced attention follows.

As you become more mindful, you might begin to see that it's possible to let your experience be as it is, without having to run a self-critical commentary around that. And more than that – perhaps you can begin to allow some encouraging self-talk to enter the picture from time to time, replacing punishing self-criticism with helpful and kindly encouragement: 'Come on, you can do this, you've got it in you. Won't it be great to pull this one off?'

Often, we make allowances for other people's humanity but we expect some kind of superhuman capacity from ourselves. But really we're all in this together – we're all frail human beings with our wants and our pains, our sadnesses and our joys. We're allowed to be human too.

Sometimes life is kind to us, at other times it's tough. With mindfulness practice, you can learn to enjoy the good things and also to accept what is challenging, staying with it – mindful and attentive – letting what is here be what is here while also navigating mindfully, making more skilful choices and heading towards more desirable outcomes.

BOX 1: WHAT IF THERE IS NO NEED TO CHANGE?

What if there is no need to change?
No need to try to transform yourself
Into someone who is more compassionate, more present,
        more loving, more wise?
How would this affect all the places in your life where you
        are endlessly trying to be better?

What if the task is simply to unfold,
To become who you already are in your essential nature:
Gentle, compassionate, and capable of living fully and
        passionately present?

What if the question is not
'Why am I so infrequently the person I really want to be?'
But 'Why do I so infrequently want to be the person
        I really am?'
How would this change what you think you have to learn?

What if becoming who and what we truly are happens
        not through striving and trying
But by recognising and receiving the people and places
        and practices
That are for us the warmth of encouragement we need to
        unfold?
How would this shape the choices you make about how
        to spend today?

What if you know that the impulse to move in a way that
    creates beauty in the world
Will arise from deep within
And guide you every time you simply pay attention
And wait?

How would this shape your stillness, your movement,
Your willingness to follow this impulse
To just let go
And dance?

USING THE BREATHING SPACE AND CHOOSING AN ACTION STEP

One of the most important practices on this course is the three-step breathing space. When challenges arise, the breathing space can make a real difference. But sometimes it won't in itself be enough to help you deal with a challenging set of circumstances. Sometimes you need to do more. There will be times when, after doing the breathing space to help you deal with a challenge, it may feel appropriate to take some considered action to help you take better care of yourself in the situation.

At such times, after the breathing space you can stay paused before re-engaging with your usual tasks and ask yourself: 'What do I most need right now? How can I best take care of myself?'

Here are some activities that may be particularly helpful at such times:

1. Do something pleasurable.
2. Do something that gives you a sense of satisfaction, achievement or control.
3. Act mindfully.

Doing Something Pleasurable

Be Kind to Your Body
- Have a nice hot bath.
- Take a nap.
- Treat yourself to some of your favourite food and don't feel guilty.
- Have your favourite hot drink.

Engage in Enjoyable Activities
- Go for a walk – alone or maybe with a dog or a friend.
- Visit a friend.
- Spend some time on your favourite hobby.
- Do some gardening.
- Take some exercise – even if only for 10 minutes.
- Phone a friend.
- Spend time with someone you like.
- Cook a meal.
- Go shopping.
- Watch something funny or engaging or uplifting on TV.
- Read something that gives you pleasure.
- Listen to music that makes you feel good.

Be aware of any killjoy thoughts that might come up here, the dour inner voice that tells you that you won't enjoy a pleasure you have planned, or that you don't deserve it, or that you should be enjoying it more. Maybe take an ironic look at such thoughts – 'Oh yes, here I go again. Undermining myself. But really, I don't need to do that – I can just let it all be.'

Do Something That Gives You a Sense of Satisfaction, Achievement or Control

- Do some housework.
- Clear out a cupboard or drawer.
- Catch up with a few emails.
- Do some routine work.
- Pay a bill.
- Do something that you have been putting off doing.
- Take some exercise.

Be aware of over-high standards and 'it should be different' thinking. Thoughts like that can make it hard for you to feel that you have achieved anything worthwhile. Notice thoughts like 'I should be doing this better/faster/more easily.' Recognise such thoughts for what they are and let them be.

When you are facing difficult times it may be helpful to break your tasks down into smaller steps and tackle them one step at a time.

Act Mindfully

When you are faced with difficulties or are feeling stressed, your mind naturally tends to be preoccupied with worries. You may be going over and over things that have happened in the past, trying to make sense of why you feel as you do, or anxiously wondering about the future. The end result is that your attention is not really on what you are doing. You become lost in your head, rather than focused on what is happening right here and now, and activities that might actually nourish you instead easily become depleting.

So when you notice that your mind has been hijacked by thoughts or feelings that take you away from the present, see what it's like to intentionally focus your entire attention on what you are doing right now. Keep your attention in each passing moment. Stay aware of your breathing as you do things; be aware of the contact of your feet with the floor as you walk; notice details like the sensation in your fingertips as you turn on the lights, the colour of the sky and clouds right now . . . Stay present.

The more powerful the thoughts and feelings you're dealing with, the more difficult this may be. But, with practice, you will find that your capacity to be more fully present in each moment will grow.

Be open-minded. Whatever you choose, treat it as an experiment. Don't prejudge how you will feel afterwards. As best you can, keep an open mind about whether doing this will be helpful in any way.

Consider a range of ways of taking care of yourself and don't limit yourself to a favourite few. Sometimes trying new behaviours can be interesting in itself. But don't expect miracles. Putting extra pressure on yourself by expecting a single activity to alter things dramatically may be unrealistic.

When you are under pressure you are more likely to revert to old habits of mind. The more mindful you are, of yourself and the world about you, the wiser your choices and actions will be.

BOX 2: STRESS – AND ITS EFFECT ON KINDNESS AND COMPASSION

In 1970, two psychologists conducted a cunningly devised experiment inspired by the parable of the Good Samaritan.

In the biblical parable, thieves beat and rob a man, leaving him naked and half dead by the side of the road. A priest passes by and crosses the road rather than help the wounded traveller. A religious functionary does the same. Then a Samaritan – from a population who was in those days thought of as one of religious outcasts – came upon the scene. He applied balm and bandages to the victim's wounds, loaded him onto a donkey, brought him to an inn, nursed him through the night and left money the following morning for the traveller's continued care.

The psychologists speculated that the parable implied that people who encounter a situation possibly calling for a helping response while thinking religious and ethical thoughts would be no more likely to offer aid than people thinking about something else. And also that those encountering a possible helping situation when they are in a hurry would be less likely to offer aid than people not so rushed.

To test those hypotheses, they gathered a sample of 40 students from the Princeton Theological Seminary. Half the students were given a copy of the parable of the Good Samaritan and told they would be required to deliver a sermon on the subject in a few minutes. The other half were told they would be talking extemporaneously about employment prospects for seminary students. All of the subjects were then told to report to an office in another building to deliver their talks. Some of them were told that they should hurry because people were waiting for them. Others were led to believe that they had slightly more time to report to the test site.

On the way to the test site, the experimenters arranged for each student to pass a poorly dressed figure slumped in a doorway, head down, eyes closed, not moving. This was deliberately an ambiguous figure: he might be in need of help, or he might be drunk and possibly dangerous – a scenario not at all unlike that of the parable. When the subjects passed, the man coughed twice and groaned.

The findings of this experiment were as the psychologists hypothesised: 60 per cent of the seminarians walked on without offering help. A seminarian thinking about the parable was no more likely to stop than one given a less lofty topic, and on several occasions a seminarian going to talk on the Good Samaritan literally stepped over the man. Only 10 per cent of those who were told to rush to the test site offered help, while 63 per cent of those who thought they had a few minutes to spare offered aid.

On further examination, the psychologists found no personality characteristics in any of the seminarians that would have led them to predict whether or not they would help. The only factor that seemed to determine the likely outcome was the degree of hurry they were in.

When we're stressed and rushing, we're less likely to help others.

BOX 3: MINDFULNESS AND COMPASSION

Another study, carried out more recently, looked at the effects of meditation training on the likelihood of people helping others. The subjects in this study were offered eight weeks of meditation instruction. Half of them undertook an MBSR course and the other half were trained in compassion. A comparison group of people who were also interested in learning meditation received the trainings after the study was complete.

At the end of their courses, the participants took various cognitive tests, believing that the experiment was measuring the effect of meditation on things like attention and memory. But the real goal of the study was to understand any changes that might have occurred in their degree of compassionate helping behaviour.

When a participant turned up for their cognitive testing at the end of the study, he or she entered a waiting room to find three chairs, two of which were occupied. What they didn't know was that the two other people in the waiting room weren't bystanders. They were 'confederates' – part of the group conducting the study.

The participant took the third seat and waited. After a minute, a third 'confederate', a woman, appeared around the corner with crutches and a walking boot. Wincing in pain as she walked, she stopped at the chairs, looked at her mobile phone, audibly sighed in discomfort and leaned back against a wall. The two other 'confederates' sat and continued to wait. This scene was allowed to play out for two more minutes.

Would the participant feel moved to respond compassionately and give up his or her chair to the woman on crutches?

As it turned out, there was a clear difference in the behaviour of the participants in the study. Those who had undergone meditation training, whether in compassion or in mindfulness, were five times more likely to give up their seat to the woman on crutches than those who had not practised meditation.

That's a huge effect. It seems that eight weeks of MBSR training can bring about a really significant increase in your levels of care and concern for others.

BOX 4: STRESS INDICATORS AND ACTION STRATEGIES

It's easy to be stressed without fully realising that. Sometimes, when we're stressed, we think thoughts like 'Oh, my life is really rubbish', but actually that's the stressed state talking. It's not an accurate description of the whole of your life. It's what things look like from the stressed perspective.

Once you understand that, you can see how useful it might be to recognise stress *as* stress. Then it's easier to see in such moments: 'Oh yes, this is stress – this isn't the whole of life; it's just me, stressed.' And, tough as it may be to feel stressed, when you know that in a sense it's *just* stress, then there are things you can do about it.

Part of your home practice this week will be to give this some thought. When you're stressed, how do you *know* you're stressed? What are your particular stress indicators?

1. Write down your own personal key stress indicators. Here are a few possible examples:

   - cramming too much in
   - an ongoing sense of compulsion
   - headaches
   - irritability
   - going to bed much later
   - sleeplessness
   - procrastination
   - tight jaw
   - churning stomach

And so on.

Take a few moments to write down your own. Then, when these show up, you're more likely to know *that* you're stressed *when* you're stressed. And that can allow you to begin to take some action to reduce your levels of stress.

Now, notice that when you're stressed you don't stop doing things. You keep on acting and some of what you do may help to alleviate your stress and some of what you do only serves to keep your stress in place. In other words, some of the actions or strategies you put in place at times of stress are helpful and some are unhelpful. If you can get clearer about this, then you stand more chance of choosing wisely when you notice that you're stressed. Of course, the same activity could be helpful or unhelpful depending on whether it's motivated by 'approach' or 'avoidance'. But you'll know the difference here by how that feels.

Take a few moments to list the unhelpful and helpful actions or strategies you tend to implement.

2. List the unhelpful strategies you tend to implement. Here are a few possible examples:

- eating too much
- not eating enough
- self-medicating with coffee, alcohol or painkillers
- unhelpful self-talk
- avoidance
- just pushing harder
- mindless television
- too much chocolate

And so on.

Take a few moments to write down your own. Then,

when you notice that you're stressed, you may be less likely to revert to one of these. After all, you know they're unhelpful.

3. List the helpful strategies you know from experience may be more effective. Here are a few possible examples:

- listening to your favourite uplifting or soothing music
- doing some physical exercise
- getting outdoors
- turning the television off, or making a definite choice about what to watch
- talking with a friend
- taking a good hot bath
- tidying the house
- eating some chocolate

And so on.

Take a few moments to write down your own. Then, when you notice that you're stressed, take a three-step breathing space and maybe implement one of these actions. Even just stepping outside for two minutes or going for a short walk can make a real difference.

BOX 5: NOURISHING AND DEPLETING ACTIVITIES

What you do with your time, from moment to moment, hour to hour, from one year to the next, deeply affects your general well-being and your ability to respond skilfully to the challenges of your life.

Try making a list of all the things you do in a fairly average day. For example:

- wake up
- first cup of tea
- meditate
- get the kids up
- lunch boxes
- breakfast
- kids off to school
- walk to bus stop

and so on . . .

Then, being as frank as you can, ask yourself: 'What, of all these things I do and take in, actually nourishes me? What energises me and makes me feel calm and centred? What increases my sense of actually being alive and present, rather than merely existing?' Put a plus (+) alongside these.

Then ask: 'Of these things that I do and take in, what depletes me? What pulls me down, drains my energy and leaves me feeling tense and fragmented? What decreases my sense of actually being alive and present? What makes me feel I am merely existing?' Put a minus (–) alongside these.

Then consider those things that are neutral – they don't bring you up, they don't bring you down. You just do them as part of your routine. Put a slash (/) alongside these.

Now, accepting that there are some aspects of your life that you simply can't change, how can you consciously choose to increase the time and effort you give to the things that nurture you?

How can you decrease the time and effort you give to the things that deplete you?

And is there any way to change some of the neutrals

into positives – to make them more nourishing and/or enjoyable?

Finally, can you learn to approach the things that at present you find depleting in a different way? Maybe by being more fully present with them, even if you find them boring or unpleasant, bringing the same curiosity and attention to them that you did with the raisin, instead of judging them or wishing that they were not there?

BOX 6: STREAM 1
HOME PRACTICE FOR WEEK SEVEN

1. Let's presume that you're going to keep up your formal mindfulness practice for at least one month after the course finishes. Then you can assess what you want to go forward with. So, from all the different forms of formal mindfulness practice that you have experienced so far in the course, use this week to settle on a form of practice that you intend to use on a regular, daily basis for the next five weeks. You might try using the audio guidance only on alternate weeks – or even less. Make your own choice about what is most helpful.
2. Practise the three-step breathing space three times a day, at times that you have decided in advance.
3. Whenever you notice unpleasant thoughts or feelings, practise the three-step breathing space to cope with the difficulty and follow that with an action step.
4. As outlined in Box 4, 'Stress Indicators and Action Strategies', list your own stress indicators. Then consider what you tend to do when stressed. What is helpful, what is unhelpful? Again, list these points. When you've done that, think about and prepare some strategies to use

when you notice one or another stress indicator in your daily life.

5. As outlined in Box 5, 'Nourishing and Depleting Activities', make a list of your daily activities, following the guidance set out there. See whether there may be any small but effective changes that you might make to the way your days unfold. Even a few apparently insignificant changes can make a tangible difference to your level of well-being.

BOX 7: STREAM 2
HOME PRACTICE FOR WEEK SEVEN

1. Let's presume that you're going to keep up your formal mindfulness practice for at least one month after the course finishes. Then you can assess what you want to go forward with. So, from all the different forms of formal mindfulness practice that you have experienced so far in the course, use this week to settle on a form of practice that you intend to use on a regular, daily basis for the next five weeks. You might try using the audio guidance only on alternate weeks – or even less. Make your own choice about what is most helpful.

2. Practise the three-step breathing space three times a day, at times that you have decided in advance.

3. Whenever you notice unpleasant thoughts or feelings, practise the three-step breathing space to cope with the difficulty and follow that with an action step.

4. As outlined in Box 4, 'Stress Indicators and Action Strategies', list your own stress indicators. Then consider what you tend to do when stressed. What is helpful, what is unhelpful? Again, list these points. When you've done

that, think about and prepare some strategies to use when you notice one or another stress indicator in your daily life.

5. As outlined in Box 5, 'Nourishing and Depleting Activities', make a list of your daily activities, following the guidance set out there. See whether there may be any small but effective changes that you might make to the way your days unfold. Even a few apparently insignificant changes can make a tangible difference to your level of well-being.

WEEK

EIGHT

LIVING
MINDFULLY

ACCEPTANCE – AND CHANGE

We're coming to the end of the course now.

Over and again throughout the course we've discussed the benefit of awareness, of an accepting and allowing attitude and of mindfully responding to situations rather than mindlessly reacting.

That mindful allowing attitude can give rise to skilful actions that bring about beneficial change. But there are also circumstances that can be very difficult, maybe even impossible, to change. There is the danger that, by carrying on trying to solve insoluble problems, or by refusing to accept the reality of the situation you are in, you can end up banging your head against a brick wall, exhausting yourself and giving rise to a sense of helplessness, stress or low mood.

In circumstances like that you can retain a sense of dignity and control by making a conscious, mindful decision *not* to try to exert control and instead to accept the situation as it is – as best you can bringing an attitude of kindness both to the situation and to your reactions to it.

As Jon Kabat-Zinn puts it, you can't stop the waves but you *can* learn to surf.

An important part of this is learning to distinguish what you can and what you cannot change.

STAYING MINDFUL

As you will have seen on the course, there are two ways of practising mindfulness. There are formal and there are informal practices. Formal practices, such as sitting meditation, body scan, yoga and so on, are key conditions in bringing about substantial inner change. There is a clear link between the amount of time spent in engaging in these practices and beneficial changes in well-being.

But informal practices have their place as well. The informal practices you will have done on the course – mindfully eating, walking, washing the dishes, brushing your teeth and so on – do not, in and of themselves, bring about the sort of changes associated with formal practice. But they do make for a richer inner life. Clearly, there is a circular relationship between formal and informal practices. When you regularly engage in formal mindfulness practice you will find that you're more inclined to pay attention to – and to enjoy – many of the simple everyday tasks you engage in.

When you live your life to the full in this way, noticing and enjoying your meals, the weather, other people and the world around you, you also find yourself more easily able to engage in formal practice. And that can help you to stay more mindful throughout your day.

The mindfulness teacher Larry Rosenberg suggests five easy steps for practising mindfulness throughout the day.

1. When possible do just one thing at a time.
2. Pay full attention to what you are doing.
3. When the mind wanders from what you are doing, bring it back.
4. Repeat Step 3 several billion times.
5. Investigate your distractions.

BOX 1: 21 WAYS TO STAY MINDFUL AT WORK

The range of possible informal practices is infinite. There is no limit to what you can pay attention to. But here is a list of possible practices that you can engage in as the working day unfolds. You might try exploring a handful of these, using this list as a general guide to spark your own ideas – changing and adapting them according to your own circumstances and temperament.

1. As you wake up, take a few moments to become aware of the world around you – the feel of the bedding, the quality of the light in the room, the sounds indoors and the sounds outside. Tune in to your breath and prepare yourself for whatever is coming next.

2. If you drink a cup of tea or coffee first thing, make that an opportunity for mindfulness practice. Take a minute or two just for yourself. Enjoy the warmth of the cup or mug, the aroma of your drink and its flavour. Gaze out of the window and take in the sounds of nature or the city – most likely, the world is waking too.

3. At the end of whatever formal practice you might do in the morning, take an extra moment or two to experience the results of the practice you've just done. Even if your mind didn't settle very easily, it's likely that you'll now be more present and alert. Savour those feelings. Don't rush.

4. If you walk to the bus, Tube or train station, make that a mindful walk. Perhaps take the chance to turn off your phone and any other communication device and give yourself over to enjoying those moments. Feel your feet on the ground and the movement in your legs and hips.

Notice how you're breathing. Allow the range of your attention to broaden and expand – take in the world around you in this moment. And if you find that your mind wanders off into the past or future, if you start to become preoccupied with the tasks ahead, remind yourself that you're allowed to take a few moments for yourself, to refresh and prepare your mind for the day to come, and bring your attention back to this moment – to the sensations, perhaps, where your feet meet the pavement and to the feelings in your legs and hips.

5. If you drive to work, take a few moments when you first get into your car just to connect with your breath and your body. Get yourself ready to drive mindfully to work.

6. As you're driving, check in from time to time and become aware of any tension that may be there: your hands tensed at the wheel, shoulders hunched, stomach clenched. Breathe into those tensions, maybe letting them soften and move. Tensing up doesn't make you a better driver.

7. Try choosing not to put on any music or not to listen to the car radio. Just be with yourself, your thoughts, feelings and body sensations as they change from moment to moment. And pay attention to the changing world outside your car. Stay in the moment and, when you find your mind wandering to the past or the future, just notice that and gently bring your attention back to the sensations of sitting there, driving.

8. See what it's like to keep to the speed limit, or just below it. It might be more relaxing. If you're driving on a motorway, what's it like to keep to the slow lane?

9. If you travel to work on a bus, Tube or train, maybe take a few moments on each journey just to tune in to yourself. Put aside the newspaper or your work, switch off your

iPod and turn off your phone. Take some time now just for yourself. Follow your breath and settle inside yourself. These are rare moments, time just for you.

10. If you park at your workplace, maybe make a point of parking further away from the entrance and give yourself the chance of a mindful walk in to work.

11. If you're using public transport, maybe get off a stop earlier and do the same. The exercise has its own obvious benefits and it's another chance to tune in to yourself and establish some mindfulness. Enjoy your walk.

12. However you got there, as you approach your office or other place of work, take a moment or two to orient yourself to the day ahead – how do you want to use this day?

13. As you sit at your desk or workstation, take a few moments from time to time to tune in to your body sensations. Notice any tension that might be there and breathe into it – softening and easing.

14. When you have a break at work, instead of reading the paper or searching on the Internet, take a real break. Get away from your computer – take a short walk and get outside if you can.

15. At lunchtime, the same applies. Get away from your desk or workstation. If you can, turn off your phone and get some air. Pause. If you meet with colleagues over lunch, try talking about things other than work from time to time.

16. Maybe eat one or two meals each week in silence. Maybe eat these meals more slowly than usual – enjoy the flavours and textures and just be with yourself.

17. Find ways of setting up mindfulness cues in your workspace. Perhaps when your phone rings you could use that as an opportunity to come back to yourself.

Maybe let it ring for a few more rings while you gather yourself before answering.

18. Before heading home, review the day. Acknowledge what you've achieved, make a list of what you need to do tomorrow and – if you can – put your work down. Maybe you've done enough for now.
19. Use your journey home as a way of making a transition. Walk or drive mindfully. Take your time.
20. As you approach your front door, prepare yourself for home and get ready to enter a different mode of life.
21. Maybe change your clothes soon after you get in and make a point of greeting everyone at home in turn. Look into their eyes and make a connection. Try taking 5 or 10 minutes to be quiet and still. If you live alone, feel what it is like to enter the quiet space of your own home, the feeling of coming into your own environment.

The ideas and practices here are just a guide. Do find your own way to be mindful at work and at home. By engaging with a few of these informal mindfulness practices each day, making them part of your routine, you can bring about significant changes to the texture and quality of each day. Just a few minutes invested every day in that way can make for huge improvements in your overall quality of life.

A life lived mindfully is so much richer and deeper.

KEEP GOING!

Now that you know the benefits of regular mindfulness practice I hope you will keep the practices up, at least to some extent as you move on from the course. Find a way of practising that works for you and do keep up the three-step breathing space whenever you need it.

Here are some tips that may be helpful as you come to establish a regular pattern of mindfulness practice in everyday life:

- If your way of life allows for routine, build your meditation or yoga practice into that routine. You probably don't need to think very much about whether or not to brush your teeth or take a shower every day. Your meditation practice can be the same once it becomes routine.
- To that end, it can help to do it at more or less the same time every day. Find out through experiment which time works best for you and then just stick to that.
- It can also help to do your practice in the same place every day. If it's possible, try setting aside a small area in your home where you can regularly do your practice. Maybe keep some fresh flowers there and your sitting-meditation gear. Even a few square metres of space would work.

Above all, remember this: you never blow it. Even if you've not done your practice for several days, even weeks, months or years – it's always there to come back to. Just sit down, close your eyes, bring your attention to your breath and there it is. It's been waiting patiently for you to return and it's as fresh as ever.

Keep going! I wish you everything of the best with that.

FURTHER RESOURCES

FURTHER TRAINING AND
OTHER RESOURCES

There is a website dedicated to this book, www.8weekmindful ness.com, which contains links and further information for those who want to explore further.

Eight-week MBSR courses are now widely available throughout the world. Details of the public courses my associates and I run in the UK can be found at www.mbsr.co.uk. The work we do in organisations is detailed at www.mindfulness-works.com.

MBSR courses are available throughout the UK and the website www.bemindful.co.uk is a good place to look for one local to you.

In the USA, the Center for Mindfulness in Medicine, Health Care, and Society is where it all started: www.umassmed.edu/ content.aspx?id=41252. They offer a range of programmes and their website offers links to a host of local practitioners in the USA and elsewhere. As they note, however, they don't vouch for the quality of these.

Google may also help to locate a course for you if you search for 'MBSR'. But beware – not everyone offering MBSR these days is qualified to do so. Check credentials carefully. If in doubt, phone the instructor and have a chat.

There are mindfulness teacher-training courses available in

different parts of the world and a Web search in your own location will be more up to date than this list could be.

The Centre for Mindfulness Research and Practice, which is part of the School of Psychology at Bangor University, is where I trained and where I sometimes teach. They offer a master's degree in mindfulness-based approaches and hold regular seven-day teacher-training retreats for those who have an established mindfulness practice. See www.bangor.ac.uk/mindfulness.

Anyone wishing to deliver mindfulness training in any setting should first of all be trained themselves, both in mindfulness and in mindfulness instruction. They should keep up their own practice and follow the 'Good Practice Guidance for Teaching Mindfulness-Based Courses' laid out below.

GOOD PRACTICE GUIDANCE FOR TEACHING MINDFULNESS-BASED COURSES

If you are interested in attending a group-based eight-week course, do check that the instructor adheres to a certain set of standards.

Here, for example, are the guidelines published by the UK Network of Mindfulness-Based Teacher Trainers in January 2010:

A. Prior Training or Relevant Background

1. Professional qualification in clinical practice, education or social context or equivalent life experience.
2. Knowledge of the populations that the mindfulness-based approach will be delivered to, including experience of teaching, therapeutic or other care provision with groups and individuals.
3. A professional mental-health training that includes the use of evidence-based therapeutic approaches (if delivering MBCT).

B. Foundational Training

1. Familiarity through personal participation with the mindfulness-based course curriculum that you will be learning to teach.
2. In-depth personal experience with daily mindfulness-meditation practice, which includes the three core practices of mindfulness-based programmes – body scan, sitting meditation and mindful movement (plus any other core practice that is a necessary part of the programme being taught, e.g. the kindly-awareness practice in the Breathworks programme).

C. Mindfulness-Based Teacher Training

1. Completion of an in-depth, rigorous mindfulness-based teacher-training programme or supervised pathway over a minimum duration of 12 months.
2. Development of awareness of the ethical framework within which you are working.
3. Development of awareness and recognition of the limitations and boundaries of your training and experience.
4. Engagement in a regular supervision process with (an) experienced mindfulness-based teacher(s) which includes:
   a. opportunity to reflect on/enquire into personal process in relation to personal mindfulness practice and mindfulness-based teaching practice;
   b. receiving periodic feedback on teaching from an experienced mindfulness-based teacher through video recordings, supervisor sitting in on teaching sessions or co-teaching and building in feedback sessions.
5. Participation in a residential teacher-led mindfulness-meditation retreat.

D. Ongoing Good Practice Requirements

1. Ongoing commitment to a personal mindfulness practice through daily formal and informal practice and attendance on retreat.
2. Ensuring that ongoing contacts with mindfulness-based colleagues are built and maintained as a means to share experiences and learn collaboratively.
3. Ongoing and regular process of supervision by (an) experienced teacher(s) of mindfulness-based approaches which includes the areas cited in C4 above.
4. Ongoing commitment to reflective practice supported by, for example, viewing recordings of own teaching sessions, connections with mindfulness teacher(s) and regular reading of books from the field of mindfulness.
5. Engaging in further training to develop skills and understanding in delivering mindfulness-based approaches.
6. A commitment to keeping up to date with the current evidence base for mindfulness-based approaches.
7. Ongoing adherence to the appropriate ethical framework of your background.

FURTHER READING

Begley, S. *Train Your Mind, Change Your Brain: How a New Science Reveals Our Extraordinary Potential to Transform Ourselves*, New York, Ballantine Books, 2007.

Burch, V., and D. Penman. *Mindfulness for Health: A Practical Guide to Relieving Pain, Reducing Stress and Restoring Well-being*, London, Piatkus, 2013.

Crane, R. *Mindfulness-Based Cognitive Therapy*, London and New York, Routledge, 2008.

Germer, C. *The Mindful Path to Self-Compassion*, London and New York, Guilford Press, 2009.

Gilbert, P. *The Compassionate Mind*, London, Constable, 2010.

Hanson, R., and R. Mendius. *Buddha's Brain: The Practical Neuroscience of Happiness, Love, and Wisdom*, Oakland, CA, New Harbinger Publications, 2009.

Heaversedge, J., and E. Halliwell. *The Mindful Manifesto: How Doing Less and Noticing More Can Help Us Thrive in a Stressed-Out World*, London, Hay House, 2012.

Kabat-Zinn, J. *Coming to Our Senses: Healing Ourselves and the World through Mindfulness*, London, Piatkus, 2005.

Kabat-Zinn, J. *Full Catastrophe Living: How to Cope with Stress, Pain and Illness Using Mindfulness Meditation*, 2nd ed., London, Piatkus, 2013.

Kabat-Zinn, J. *Wherever You Go, There You Are: Mindfulness Meditation for Everyday Life*, London, Piatkus, 2004.

Segal, Z.V., J.M.G. Williams and J.D. Teasdale. *Mindfulness-Based*

Cognitive Therapy for Depression: A New Approach to Preventing Relapse, 2nd ed., London, Guilford Press, 2012.

Siegel, D.J. The Mindful Brain: Reflection and Attunement in the Cultivation of Well-Being, New York, W.W. Norton, 2007.

Teasdale, J., M. Williams and Z. Segal. The Mindful Way Workbook: An 8-Week Program to Free Yourself from Depression and Emotional Distress, London, Guilford Press, 2013.

Wax, R. Sane New World: Taming the Mind, London, Hodder & Stoughton, 2013.

Williams, M., and D. Penman. Mindfulness: A Practical Guide to Finding Peace in a Frantic World, London, Piatkus, 2011.

Williams, M., J. Teasdale, Z. Segal and J. Kabat-Zinn. The Mindful Way through Depression: Freeing Yourself from Chronic Unhappiness, London and New York, Guilford Press, 2007.

NOTES

INTRODUCTION

Page 6
Jon Kabat-Zinn (of whom more later) speaks of it as the awareness that arises from paying attention on purpose, in the present moment and non-judgementally: this is based on Jon Kabat-Zinn's description, found in *Wherever You Go, There You Are: Mindfulness Meditation for Everyday Life*, New York, Hyperion, 1994, p. 4.

Page 10
Towards the end of the nineteenth century that began to change as European explorers, scholars and colonial administrators began to discover and translate into their own contexts some of what was going on in Asian monasteries: P.C. Almond, *The British Discovery of Buddhism*, Cambridge, Cambridge University Press, 1988.

Page 11
'What shall I do with my life? What kind of work do I love so much I would pay to do it?': Jon Kabat-Zinn, 'Some reflections on the origins of MBSR, skilful means, and the trouble with maps', *Contemporary Buddhism*, vol. 12/1 (2011), pp. 281–306.

Page 11
What, he wondered, was the system offering to the other 80 per cent?: this is taken from a comment Jon made on a PBS television

show presented by Bill Moyers in 1993. The programme is written up in B. Moyers, *Healing and the Mind*, New York, Broadway Books, 1993, and it is available to watch on YouTube – search there for 'Healing and the Mind'.

Page 13

More than 740 academic medical centres, hospitals, clinics and freestanding programmes offer MBSR to the public around the world: Jon Kabat-Zinn, 'No blueprint, just love', *Mindful* magazine, February 2014, p. 36.

Page 13

the symptoms of those who engaged in the MBSR course along-side that treatment cleared up around 50 per cent faster than the symptoms of patients who didn't: J. Kabat-Zinn *et al.*, 'Influence of a mindfulness meditation-based stress reduction intervention on rates of skin clearing in patients with moderate to severe psoriasis undergoing phototherapy (UVB) and photochemotherapy (PUVA)', *Psychosomatic Medicine*, vol. 60/5 (1998), pp. 625–32.

Page 13

travelled to Dharamsala in the foothills of the Indian Himalayas on a kind of neuroscience expedition: S. Begley, *Train Your Mind, Change Your Brain: How a New Science Reveals Our Extraordinary Potential to Transform Ourselves*, New York, Ballantine Books, 2007.

Page 15

asked by the director of a clinical psychology research network to develop a group-based therapy for the treatment of relapsing depression: Z.V. Segal *et al.*, *Mindfulness-Based Cognitive Therapy for Depression: A New Approach to Preventing Relapse*, 2nd ed., London, Guilford Press, 2012.

Page 15
a World Health Organization projection suggests that of all diseases depression will impose the second-largest burden of ill health worldwide by the year 2020: Z.V. Segal et al., *Mindfulness-Based Cognitive Therapy for Depression: A New Approach to Preventing Relapse*, 2nd ed., London, Guilford Press, 2012.

Page 15
when people have had three or more serious episodes of depression there is something like a 67 per cent chance that their depression will relapse: Z.V. Segal et al., *Mindfulness-Based Cognitive Therapy for Depression: A New Approach to Preventing Relapse*, 2nd ed., London, Guilford Press, 2012.

Page 16
Mary has just come from work: Z.V. Segal et al., *Mindfulness-Based Cognitive Therapy for Depression: A New Approach to Preventing Relapse*, 2nd ed., London, Guilford Press, 2012, pp. 33–4.

Page 18
The simple act of recognising your thoughts as thoughts can free you from the distorted reality they often create and allow for more clear-sightedness and a greater sense of manageability in your life: J. Kabat-Zinn, *Full Catastrophe Living: How to Cope with Stress, Pain and Illness Using Mindfulness Meditation*, 2nd ed., London, Piatkus, 2013. p. 66.

Page 19
obsessive-compulsive disorder, disordered eating, addiction, traumatic brain injury, obesity and bipolar disorder among others: Z.V. Segal et al., *Mindfulness-Based Cognitive Therapy for Depression: A New Approach to Preventing Relapse*, 2nd ed., London, Guilford Press, 2012.

Page 19

if relapse does occur, those who have trained in MBCT appear to experience it less severely: J. Piet and E. Hougaard, 'The effect of mindfulness-based cognitive therapy for prevention of relapse in recurrent major depressive disorder: a systematic review and meta-analysis', *Clinical Psychology Review*, vol. 31/6 (2011), pp. 1032–40.

Page 20

I came upon a master's degree programme that was being run at Bangor University in Wales: see www.bangor.ac.uk/mindfulness.

Page 23

I wrote a book on this theme: M. Chaskalson, *The Mindful Workplace*, Oxford, Wiley-Blackwell, 2011.

Page 23

an executive master's in positive leadership and strategy (EXMPLS), which has mindfulness training at its heart: see http://exmpls.ie.edu for more information about this programme.

Page 24

recommends it as a front-line treatment in instances of relapsing depression: National Institute for Health and Clinical Excellence, *Depression: The Treatment and Management of Depression in Adults* (2009), a partial update of NICE clinical guideline 23, retrieved 6 September 2013 from www.nice.org.uk/nicemedia/pdf/cg90niceguideline.pdf.

Page 24

The United States Marine Corps, on the other hand, has found that it helps soldiers remain mentally flexible, cognitively clear and emotionally appropriate under pressure: A.P. Jha et al.,

'Examining the protective effects of mindfulness training on working memory capacity and affective experience', *Emotion*, vol. 1 (2010), pp. 54–64.

Page 24
Peer-reviewed research papers are currently emerging at a rate of around 40 per month: see www.mindfulexperience.org for a list of thousands of mindfulness research papers. For a systematic review of the evidence, see A. Chiesa and A. Serretti, 'A systematic review of neurobiological and clinical features of mindfulness meditations', *Psychological Medicine*, vol. 40/8 (2010), pp. 1239–52.

Page 24
Their 2010 Mindfulness Report: www.livingmindtully.co.uk/downloads/Mindfulness_Report.pdf.

Page 26
increased brain grey-matter concentration in areas connected with sustained attention, emotional regulation and perspective taking: B.K. Hölzel *et al.*, 'Mindfulness practice leads to increases in regional brain gray matter density', *Psychiatry Research: Neuroimaging*, vol. 191/1 (2011), pp. 36–43.

Page 26
increased cortical thickness: S.W. Lazar *et al.*, 'Meditation experience is associated with increased cortical thickness', *Neuroreport*, vol. 16/17 (2005), pp. 1893–7.

Page 26
decreased amygdala activation: the amygdala is a key component in the brain's threat-detection system – when it is less active you feel more at ease with yourself and others. See J.J. Cresswell *et al.*,

'Neural correlates of dispositional mindfulness during affect labeling', *Psychosomatic Medicine*, vol. 69 (2007), pp. 560–65.

Page 27
if the left prefrontal is more active then you're likely to experience higher levels of well-being: R.J. Davidson *et al.*, 'Alterations in brain and immune function produced by mindfulness meditation', *Psychosomatic Medicine*, vol. 65 (2003), pp. 564–70.

Page 27
It is also a key component in emotion regulation and it is reduced by acute or chronic stress: A.P. Jha *et al.*, 'Examining the protective effects of mindfulness training on working memory capacity and affective experience', *Emotion*, vol. 10/1 (2010), pp. 54–64.

Page 27
programmes for schoolchildren and young adults, like: http:// mindfulnessinschools.org.

Page 27
the programme developed by my colleagues at Bangor University: www.bangor.ac.uk/mindfulness/education.php.en.

Page 27
how many people in the room think that regular physical training can be crucial for their health and well-being: I discovered these questions watching a YouTube video by the wonderful Amishi Jha who studies the neuroscience of mindfulness.

Page 27
even as late as 1970, when the New York City marathon was first run with 127 entrants: www.nyrr.org/about-us/marathon-history.

Page 27

a world record for a marathon race: www.tcsnycmarathon.org.

WEEK ONE

Page 38

and this is a wonderful capacity: W. Schneider and R.M. Shiffrin, 'Controlled and automatic human information processing: detection, search, and attention', *Psychological Review*, vol. 84/1 (1977), pp. 1–66.

Page 46

Novak Djokovic, one of the world's most formidable tennis players, uses yoga and meditation to keep himself in good physical, mental and emotionul shape: www.telegraph.co.uk/sport/tennis/novakdjokovic/10149230/Novak-Djokovic-taps-into-the-power-of-Buddha-for-inner-peace-during-Wimbledon-2013.html.

Page 47

Before doing the body scan, try this very brief exercise, right now, for a few moments: I'm grateful to my colleague Ciaran Saunders for introducing me to this exercise.

Page 54

Like Mister Duffy in James Joyce's The Dubliners *who 'lived a little distance from his body'*: J. Joyce, *The Dubliners*, London, Penguin Modern Classics, 2000.

WEEK TWO

Page 80

In no particular order, here are a number of attitudinal qualities associated with mindfulness training that I hope will begin to emerge for you as you engage with this course: this list is adapted from one published in S. Shapiro and L. Carlson, *The Art and Science of Mindfulness: Integrating Mindfulness into Psychology and the Helping Professions*, Washington, DC, American Psychological Association, 2008.

WEEK THREE

Page 93

In a famous study conducted in 1988: F. Strack *et al.*, 'Inhibiting and facilitating conditions of the human smile: a nonobtrusive test of the facial feedback hypothesis', *Journal of Personality and Social Psychology*, vol. 54/5 (1988), pp. 768–77.

Page 95

even if you engage in regular daily exercise: H.P. van der Ploeg *et al.*, 'Sitting time and all-cause mortality risk in 222,497 Australian adults', *Archives of Internal Medicine*, vol. 172/6 (2012), pp. 494–500.

Page 127

The results that emerged from Davidson's studies with the monks were extreme: S. Begley, *Train Your Mind, Change Your Brain: How a New Science Reveals Our Extraordinary Potential to Transform Ourselves*, New York, Ballantine Books, 2007.

Page 128

They delivered an eight-week mindfulness course to workers in a high-pressure biotech company in Madison, Wisconsin: R.J. Davidson *et al.*, 'Alterations in brain and immune function produced by mindfulness meditation', *Psychosomatic Medicine*, vol. 65 (2003), pp. 564–70.

Page 129

For an empiricist, that was enough: http://events.nytimes.com/2003/09/14/magazine/14BUDDHISM.html.

Pages 129–30

For simplicity's sake we might call these the avoidance system (for BIS) and the approach system (for BAS): J.A. Gray, 'A critique of Eysenck's theory of personality', in *A Model for Personality*, ed. H.J. Eysenck, Berlin, Springer-Verlag, 1981 pp. 246–76.

Page 131

our forebears lived in tribal bands – usually no bigger than 150 members: A. Norenzayan and A.F. Shariff, 'The origin and evolution of religious prosociality', *Science*, vol. 332 (2008), pp. 58–62.

Page 131

we have the capacity to sense – and to simulate within our own experience – other people's actions, their emotions and their thoughts: R. Hanson and R. Mendius, *Buddha's Brain: The Practical Neuroscience of Happiness, Love, and Wisdom*, Oakland, CA, New Harbinger Publications, 2009.

Pages 131–2

That gives you, in your own body, a felt sense of what others experience in their bodies: S.D. Preston and F.B.M. de Waal,

'Empathy: its ultimate and proximate bases', *Behavioral and Brain Sciences*, vol. 25 (2002), pp. 1–72.

Page 132
That allows you to make sense of the feelings of others: T. Singer *et al.*, 'Empathy for pain involves the affective but not sensory components of pain', *Science*, vol. 303 (2004), pp. 1157–62.

Page 132
Together, these produce your overall perception of their inner experience: T. Singer, 'The neuronal basis and ontogeny of empathy and mind reading: review of literature and implications for future research', *Neuroscience and Biobehavioral Reviews*, vol. 30 (2006), pp. 855–63.

Page 132
The capacity for two people to 'feel felt': D.J. Siegel, *The Mindful Brain: Reflection and Attunement in the Cultivation of Well-Being*, New York, W.W. Norton, 2007.

Page 133
Drawing on a variety of research findings, he notes: www.norman farb.com/research.

Page 134
In 2007 Farb and his colleagues published a study: N.A. Farb *et al.*, 'Attending to the present: mindfulness meditation reveals distinct neural modes of self-reference', *SCAN*, vol. 2 (2007), pp. 313–22.

WEEK FOUR

Page 170

A survey of the US population in 1973: Bruskin Associates, cited in *Spectra*, vol. 9/6 (1973), p. 4.

WEEK FIVE

Page 187

The easiest way to relax is to stop trying to make things different: J. Goldstein, *Insight Meditation: The Practice of Freedom*, Boston, Shambhala, 2003, p. 39.

Page 189

he found himself on a training course, preparing to give a talk on the way in which craving and aversion drive human suffering: J.D. Teasdale and M. Chaskalson, 'How does mindfulness transform suffering? I: the nature and origins of *dukkha*', *Contemporary Buddhism*, vol. 12/1 (2011), pp. 89–102.

WEEK SIX

Page 198

After all, it wasn't part of a caretaker's duty: Z.V. Segal et al., *Mindfulness-Based Cognitive Therapy for Depression: A New Approach to Preventing Relapse*, 2nd ed., London, Guilford Press, 2012, p. 299.

Page199

Consider another two very brief scenarios now, outlined below: Z.V. Segal et al., *Mindfulness-Based Cognitive Therapy for Depression: A New Approach to Preventing Relapse*, 2nd ed., London, Guilford Press, 2012.

Page 206

This is an expression of our innate wisdom and compassion: J. Kabat-Zinn, *Full Catastrophe Living: How to Cope with Stress, Pain and Illness Using Mindfulness Meditation*, 2nd ed., London, Piatkus, 2013, pp. 66–8.

Page 206

The writer Valerie Cox: Valerie Cox, in *A 3rd Serving of Chicken Soup for the Soul: 101 More Stories to Open the Heart and Rekindle the Spirit*, ed. J. Canfield and M. V. Hansen, HCI, Florida, 1996, p. 199.

Page 207

The meditation teacher Joseph Goldstein uses the analogy of a train to describe this process: J. Goldstein, *Insight Meditation: The Practice of Freedom*, Boston, Shambhala, 2003.

Page 211

Three Strategies for Dealing with Distress: J.D. Teasdale and M. Chaskalson, 'How does mindfulness transform suffering? II: the transformation of *dukkha*', *Contemporary Buddhism*, vol. 12/1 (2011), pp. 103–24.

WEEK SEVEN

Page 220

The nature of mindfulness is engagement; where there is interest, a natural, unforced attention follows: C. Feldman, *The Buddhist Path to Simplicity: Spiritual Practice for Everyday Life*, London, Thorsons, p.173.

Pages 221–2

To just let go / And dance: Oriah Mountain Dreamer, from the prelude to *The Dance*, New York, HarperCollins, 2001.

Page 225

In 1970, two psychologists conducted a cunningly devised experiment inspired by the parable of the Good Samaritan: J.M. Darley and C.D. Batson, 'From Jerusalem to Jericho: a study of situational and dispositional variables in helping behavior', *Journal of Personality and Social Psychology*, vol. 27 (1973), pp. 100–108.

Page 227

Another study, carried out more recently, looked at the effects of meditation training on the likelihood of people helping others: P. Condon *et al.*, 'Meditation increases compassionate responses to suffering', *Psychological Science*, vol. 24 (2013), pp. 2125–7.

WEEK EIGHT

Page 239
As Jon Kabat-Zinn puts it, you can't stop the waves but you can learn to surf: Wherever You Go, There You Are: Mindfulness Meditation for Everyday Life, New York, Hyperion, 1994, p. 30.

Page 240
There is a clear link between the amount of time spent in engaging in these practices and beneficial changes in well-being: J. Carmody and R.A. Baer, 'Relationships between mindfulness practice and levels of mindfulness, medical and psychological symptoms and well-being in a Mindfulness-Based Stress Reduction program', *Journal of Behavioural Medicine*, vol. 31 (2008), pp. 23–33.

Page 240
Investigate your distractions: L. Rosenberg, *Breath by Breath: The Liberating Practice of Insight Meditation*, Boston, Shambhala, 1998, pp. 168–70.

Page 241
But here is a list of possible practices: S.F. Santorelli, 'Mindfulness and mastery in the workplace', in *Engaged Buddhist Reader*, ed. A. Kotler, Berkeley, Parallax Press, 1996, pp. 39–45.

INDEX

Page references in italics denote diagrams.

LIST OF AUDIO FILES

(DOWNLOAD AT www.mbsr.co.uk/mp31.php)

Track	Title	Minutes
1	The Raisin Exercise	15
2	The Body Scan (Longer Version)	35
3	The Body Scan (Shorter Version)	15
4	Mindfulness of Breathing (10-Minute Version)	10
5	Mindfulness of Breathing (5-Minute Version)	5
6	Mindful Movement (Longer Version)	35
7	Mindful Movement (Shorter Version)	15
8	Three-Step Breathing Space	3
9	Walking Meditation	10
10	Mindfulness of the Breath and Body	10
11	Mindfulness of Sounds and Thoughts	10
12	Choiceless Awareness	10
13	Sitting with the Difficult	10
14	40 Minute Sitting Meditation	40
15	30 Minute Sitting Meditation	30
16	20 Minute Sitting Meditation	20
17	30 Minutes 'Sitting with the Difficult' Meditation	30
18	20 Minutes 'Sitting with the Difficult' Meditation	20

ABOUT THE AUTHOR

Michael has taught the course outlined in this book to thousands of people.

He has a master's degree in the clinical applications of mindfulness and 40 years of personal practice of mindfulness and related disciplines. He has delivered mindfulness training in courses throughout the world, in public courses or to groups and individuals in organisations – including a number of global corporations, the UK's National Health Service, its civil service and several leading business schools.

Michael is an honorary lecturer at Bangor University, where he taught for several years on the master's degree programme run by the Centre for Mindfulness Research and Practice in the School of Psychology. He is also an adjunct professor at IE Business School in Madrid, where he teaches mindful leadership practices.

Michael's work is deeply informed by his own mindfulness practice and his knowledge of the contemporary research – including cutting-edge neuroscience research – into the use of mindfulness in a wide variety of contexts.

Michael is based in Cambridge, UK, and travels extensively.

ACKNOWLEDGEMENTS

Ciaran Saunders, Jane Brendgen and Mark McMordie all read the text and made helpful comments. Any errors and omissions, however, are mine.

I am grateful to my colleagues at the Centre for Mindfulness Research and Practice at Bangor University and to Juan Humberto Young who leads the EXMPLS programme at IE Business School for their support and co-teaching – I have learned so much from all of them. And I am hugely thankful to John Teasdale and Ciaran Saunders for the many stimulating conversations we have had around mindfulness and related themes. Long may these continue.

Josie Harrison has taken on running the Mindfulness Works public courses in a way that has left me completely free to focus on writing and teaching. Thank you Jo. And I have been able to confidently leave my diary and complex travel arrangements in the able hands of my assistant Rachel Guyat. A huge relief.

Besides reading the text in great detail, my wife, Annette Chaskalson, has been a constant and loving support as I've tried to negotiate a packed teaching and writing schedule and get this book done to deadline. For that and so much else, thank you my love.

PERMISSIONS

Permission was granted to reprint text from the following:

The Essential Rumi
Coleman Barks & John Moyne
0-062-50959-4
Selection: The Guest House
HarperOne

There's a Hole in My Sidewalk: The Romance of Self-Discovery
Portia Nelson
0-941-83187-6
Selection: Autobiography in Five Short Chapters
Simon & Schuster

The Dance: Moving to the Deep Rhythms of Your Life
Oriah Mountain Dreamer
0-061-11670-X
Selection: What if there is no need to change?
HarperOne

Full Catastrophe Living
Jon Kabat-Zinn
0-749-95841-3
Piatkus Books